THE DAVID HUME INSTITUTE 1989

AGATHOTOPIA:
THE ECONOMICS OF PARTNERSHIP

GW00578245

THE DAVID HUME INSTITUTE 1989

Agathotopia:
The Economics of Partnership

J E Meade

A Tract for the Times Addressed to All Capitalists
and Socialists who Seek to Make the Best of Both Worlds

ABERDEEN UNIVERSITY PRESS

First published 1989
Aberdeen University Press
A member of the Pergamon Group
© The David Hume Institute

*All rights reserved. Except as permitted under current legislation
no part of this work may be photocopied, stored in a retrieval system,
published, performed in public, adapted, broadcast, recorded or reproduced
in any form or by any means, without prior permission of the copyright
owner. Enquiries should be addressed to Aberdeen University Press
Farmers Hall, Aberdeen.*

British Library Cataloguing in Publication Data
Meade, J E (James Edward), *1907–*
Agathotopia.
1. Great Britain. Companies. Management.
Participation of personnel
I. Title   II. David Hume Institute
658.3′152′0941

ISBN 0 08 037967 2

PRINTED IN GREAT BRITAIN
THE UNIVERSITY PRESS
ABERDEEN

Contents

Biographical Note

JAMES EDWARD MEADE, CB, Nobel Laureate in Economics is Emeritus Professor of Political Economy at the University of Cambridge. His distinguished career as an economist began as a Fellow of Hertford College, Oxford in the 1930s. He was one of the senior economists in Government during World War Two, becoming Director of the Economic Section of the Cabinet. For ten years (1947–57) he was Professor of Commerce (with special reference to International Trade) at the London School of Economics and Political Science, before becoming Professor of Political Economy at the University of Cambridge (1957–68) and a Fellow of Christ's College (1957–74). Among his many publications, those closely related to this Hume Paper include: *Planning and the Price Mechanism* (1948), *Efficiency, Equality and the Ownership of Property* (1964), *The Just Economy* (1976), and *The Intelligent Radical's Guide to Economic Policy* (1975).

Professor Meade has received many honours which recognise his outstanding contributions to economics, including Presidency of the Royal Economic Society (1964–66) and that unique accolade, The Nobel Prize in Economics (1977). He was awarded the Companionship of the Order of the Bath for his service in the Cabinet Office.

Foreword

Economists have long debated whether or not a capitalist system is compatible with an acceptable distribution of income and with harmony of interests between workers and capitalists. At one extreme have been hard-line Marxists who have claimed that nothing short of state capital ownership will fulfil these aims, whereas, at the other extreme, 'Austrian' economists have maintained that a competitive capitalist system will achieve these objectives but only if it is free from government intervention. At a rough guess it could reasonably be claimed that most western economists of repute would maintain an intermediate position with the distribution of their views along the political spectrum somewhat biased towards support for a free market economy of capitalist profit-making enterprises but one in which the government had a significant part to play in influencing income distribution and in regulating conditions of work.

A few major economists have sought the solution to the problem of economic conflict in the breaking up of the traditional mould of a hierarchical system of business organisation. 'The form of association . . . which if mankind continue to improve must be expected in the end to predominate is not that which can exist between capitalist as chief and work-people without a voice in the management, but the association of the labourers themselves on terms of equality, collectively owning the capital with which they carry on their operations and working under managers, elected and removable by themselves'. So wrote John Stuart Mill in 1871. In recent years, a burgeoning literature in economic analysis have investigated Mill's 'dream', much of it governed by the hope that labour-managed enterprises could be demonstrated to be at least as efficient as capitalist ones, but with the additional satisfaction to workers that they controlled their own destiny. Very broadly speaking, the verdict of 'not proven' seems to be the correct label to attach to these demonstrations. In particular, it has been shown that if firms attempt to maximise the average earnings per worker in the business, an economy of labour-managed enterprises with an increasing working population might be characterised by growing unemployment; for it would not be in the interests of those already in employment to expand output by expanding employment. This undesired result suggests that careful attention has to be paid to the precise rules which should govern the operation of such enterprises.

The author of *Agathotopia*, Professor James Meade, is one of the outstanding economists of this century, and one of only four British economists who have become Nobel Laureates in Economics. Throughout a long career as an economic theorist, who has made major contributions to international trade theory and macroeconomic theory and policy, he has repeatedly returned to the question of the ideal organisation of economic life. As the reader will soon discover, his pursuit of this question is not governed merely by intellectual curiosity but by his profound concern for the welfare of his fellow men.

Professor Meade relates that he has discovered the answer to the problem of reconciling capitalism and socialism by a journey in search of Utopia— the Perfect Place (strictly speaking 'no place')—but instead he found Agathotopia—the Good Place which has essayed the more modest task of producing good institutions for imperfect people. The Agathotopians, as explained by their spokesman, Dr Semaj Edaem (whose name will somehow seem familiar to the reader), have developed, not without difficulty, a novel form of worker-capitalist partnership in which both workers and capitalists share the risks, but special fiscal arrangements ensure that income and wealth do not become intolerably unequal and the poor and unfortunate are cared for without humiliating enquiry into their circumstances. The retailing of their views by Professor Meade is compelling. Summarising them would not do them justice and is in any case unnecessary, given his well known powers of exposition. One suspects, however, that the Agathotopians who appear to be a thoughtful people, have not resisted the importation and adoption of ideas originating with the scholarly works of a Professor formerly at, to use the Agathotopian form, the University of Nodnol and latterly at the University of Egdir-Bmac.

The Agathotopian interest has extended to the elaboration of some of their major propositions in mathematical form. Professor Meade has performed the additional service of satisfying those readers who prefer this alternative mode of exposition.

I suspect that readers of Hume Papers may be sharply divided in their opinions of the acceptability of Agathotopian economic institutions, but united in their admiration of the skilful presentation of the Agathotopian case by the author. The Institute has no collective view on policy matters, but feels particularly privileged to act as Professor Meade's vehicle of publication. David Hume, to be sure, would have applauded his approach having himself sought to outline the political rather than the economic organisation which would form 'The Idea of a Perfect Commonwealth'—one of his superb essays. He wrote: 'all plans of government, which suppose great reformation in the manners of mankind are plainly imaginary' which is why he found Utopia wanting and preferred Harrington's Oceana. Like James Meade, he saw his task as that of designing 'good' institutions for imperfect beings. Only great minds are equal to such a task.

ALAN PEACOCK
Executive Director

Preface

In March 1988, the Italian 'Lega Nazionale delle Cooperative e Mutue' (League of Cooperative Societies) held a two-day conference in Rome. They were concerned with the problem of introducing equity capital into their cooperative societies and for this purpose were considering the possibility of admitting capital-providing members as well as labour-providing members. This they wished to do without compromising their cooperative spirit and without losing their legal status as cooperatives which gave them certain tax privileges. The strict purpose of the conference was to consider this particular problem and the second day of the conference was devoted to its discussion.

But the conference had also a broader theme. The organisers and promoters of the conference were convinced of the merits of a competitive market economy but, like so many members of the moderate left in politics, were much concerned with the question whether and, if so, in which way principles of compassion, equality, antipoverty, and social responsibility could at the same time be incorporated in the system. In particular could the cooperative movement help to provide the answer? Dr Edwin Morley-Fletcher of the University of Rome, a principal adviser of Mr Turci, the President of Lega, was familiar with my ideas about Labour-Capital Partnerships and about the organisation of economies which paid attention to equality and participation as well as to incentives for efficiency. Accordingly I was invited to the conference and was given the opportunity on the first day to express my views at the morning session on the organisation of Labour-Capital Partnerships and at the afternoon session to open a panel discussion on the general characteristics of an economy in which such a partnership principle might flourish.

Parts II and III of the present tract, on the Partnership Enterprise and the Partnership Economy respectively, cover the grounds of my talks at the morning and at the afternoon sessions of this conference.[1] The interest shown in these ideas has led to their publication in an Italian translation in the form of a book covering the present tract together with an introduction by Dr Edwin Morley-Fletcher.[2]

The reader of the present tract should bear in mind that its origin has greatly affected the range of subjects which it discusses. The Rome conference was about the possibility of organising individual enterprises on cooperative principles which accepted the providers of capital as full cooperators and about the background of fiscal and other arrangements which would mitigate any undesirable effects upon risk-bearing or upon the distribution of income and wealth. Thus there is a very wide range of economic features of a good society with which the present tract does not treat. The control of pollution and other external economies and diseconomies, the case for and against central State planning of certain activities, and the economic and financial relations between different countries are outstanding examples. It should in particular be noted that the present tract does not even touch upon the basic problem of the control of monopolistic practices. Competitive arrangements are advocated wherever possible, but no proposals are made about the treatment of various degrees of monopoly in those cases where inevitably monopolistic conditions prevail.[3]

I realised that I was being foolhardy in talking to a conference of the Italian cooperative movement in total ignorance of any of the distinctive features and problems of that movement. It was, therefore, totally inappropriate for me to deal with specific detailed arrangements. It was largely for this reason that I cast my remarks in the fanciful form of a visit to another community which had solved the basic problems—a country which had in fact devised 'the best of all possible arrangements' with due emphasis on the word 'possible'.[4]

I hope very much that this particular form of presentation will not hide the fact that it is serious possibilities which are at issue. I do not, of course, believe that one could introduce the whole structure discussed in this tract without selection and modification and without the historical experience of much slow trial and error. But both the ideas underlying Part II on the Partnership Enterprise and Part III on the Partnership Economy are of great relevance in the present world, in which on one side of the Iron Curtain much thought is being given to the introduction of participatory market competitive enterprises into a command economy and on the other side many are searching for ways to introduce organised social responsibility for greater compassion and equality into a system of unbridled individual competitive money-making. The present time offers a golden opportunity for a constructive exchange of basic ideas.

In revising the text for this tract I am much indebted to comments made by Dr Edwin Morley-Fletcher, Professor Mario Nuti, Dr Jeremy Edwards and Mr Martin Weale. I am grateful to Professor Sir Henry Phelps Brown for a powerful exposition of the obstacles which human relations between owners, managers and workers may well put in the way of the successful development of Labour–Capital Partnerships; but I have confined myself in this tract to a discussion of the institutional–structural arrangements which would give the best chance for their successful operation. The virtues of the macroeconomic arrangements discussed in Part III of this tract remain relevant however limited may be the growth of participatory enterprises in the competitive sector of the economy.

J E Meade,
Christ's College,
Cambridge.
February 1989

Part I Introduction

I recently set sail to visit the island of Utopia which, I have been told, constitutes a Perfect Place to live in. But, alas, I could find the island Nowhere. However on my way home I chanced to visit the nearby island of Agathotopia. The inhabitants made no claim for perfection in their social arrangements, but they did claim the island to be a Good Place to live in. I studied their institutions closely, came to the conclusion that their social arrangements were indeed about as good as one could hope to achieve in this wicked world, and returned home to recommend Agathotopian arrangements for my own country.

I am making Agathotopian rather than Utopian recommendations simply because I could not find Utopia. But the reason why I could not find that island was something of a mystery. The Agathotopians seemed to have no basically hostile feelings towards their Utopian neighbours, but were very secretive about them and strangely unwilling to help me to find the island. I was very puzzled until some remarks by the rather decrepit Agathotopian economist Professor Dr Semaj Edaem inadvertently suggested to me the following explanation of their reserved attitude to the Utopians.

The Utopians have, I suspect, gone in for genetic engineering in a big way and have produced a race of perfect human beings. The Agathotopians are in many ways a conservative lot and have been either unable or, as I suspect, unwilling to follow Plato in taking the necessary measures to breed genetically a race of people with inborn perfect social behaviour. The Utopians, if I am right, have the task of producing perfect institutions for perfect human beings; the Agathotopians have tried only to produce good institutions for imperfect people.

If this is the explanation of the Agathotopian attitude towards the Utopians, my study of Agathotopia suggests a very important connection between institutions and behaviour. The Agathotopians have devised institutions which rely very largely on self-centred enterprising behaviour in a free competitive market but which, at the same time, put great stress upon cooperation between individuals in producing the best possible outcome and upon a compassionate attitude to those who would otherwise lose out. The typical Agathotopian has a more cooperative and compassionate attitude in his or her social behaviour than is the case at present in the United Kingdom, where we have, alas, been subject for so many years to such a regime of devil-take-the-hindmost and grab-as-much-money-as-quickly-as-possible. This suggests that there is some positive feedback between social institutions and social attitudes.

If this interpretation is true, it means that it will be difficult at first for us to enjoy the advantages of Agathotopian institutions until there has been time for the positive feedbacks between institutions and attitudes to operate effectively. But there is also the implication that it may not be a waste of time to make Agathotopian institutional changes which are somewhat out of harmony with present attitudes, but may well in time help to mould these attitudes in the desired direction.

Part II The Partnership Enterprise

At the level of the individual competitive business enterprise the Agatho-topians have encouraged the formation of what they call Discriminating Labour-Capital Partnerships.

A Pure Form of Labour-Capital Partnership

The easiest way to explain the basic idea of such a partnership between labour and capital is to imagine it to be suddenly applied to an existing firm in a completely undiluted form. Consider then a Capitalist Company of the familiar kind. Suppose that of its revenue 80 per cent is being paid to the employees and the remaining 20 per cent is accruing to the capitalists. Simple conversion of this into a pure Labour-Capital Partnership would consist of the issue of two kinds of Share Certificates, namely:

1   Capital Share Certificates which would be distributed to all the persons who were in fact receiving directly, or indirectly through profit, interest, rent etc, the capitalists' 20 per cent share of the firm's revenue, this distribution to each beneficiary being *pro rata* to his or her existing income from the business; and
2   Labour Share Certificates which would be distributed to all employees *pro rata* to their individual earnings of the remaining 80 per cent of the firm's revenue.

All Share Certificates, whether Capital or Labour, would carry an entitlement to the same rate of dividend.

   The immediate result of this conversion would be that everyone concerned would receive an unchanged income, but in every case in the form of a dividend on a share-holding, which would replace all interest, rent, wages, etc; but everyone concerned in the operation of the business would now have a share in the future success or failure of the enterprise.

   There would, however, be one basic distinction between Capital Share Certificates and Labour Share Certificates. Capital Share Certificates would correspond more or less exactly to a Capitalist Company's existing Ordinary

3

Shares. They could be freely traded on the Stock Exchange or elsewhere in the market and could be transferred from one owner to the other.

Labour Share Certificates on the other hand would be tied to the individual working partner and would be surrendered and cancelled when he or she retired or voluntarily left the business. They would not, however, be cancelled if the worker left the partnership involuntarily (e.g. because of redundancy), unless the dismissal was due to grave misconduct or illness which incapacitated the worker for the job. The worker would thus normally be guaranteed employment, or at least an appropriate share of income from employment until retirement. His or her claim on the firm would, however, be tied to availability to perform the work for which the dividend on Labour Share Certificates was the reward. There could, of course, as now be separate pension arrangements for those who had retired, together with separate arrangements for the support of worker partners in ill health.

In a similar manner an existing Labour-Managed Cooperative which had raised all its capital funds in the form of fixed interest debt and in which the working members of the cooperative shared the net revenue produced by the cooperative could be transformed into a Labour-Capital Partnership. The fixed interest debt would be transformed into holdings of Capital Share Certificates with an initial rate of dividend which provided the same income as before to those who had provided the capital funds; and the existing distribution of the cooperative's net revenue among the working cooperators would be transformed into individual holdings of Labour Share Certificates in such amounts that the initial rate of dividend would provide an unchanged income to each individual cooperator.

A Capitalist Company owned by persons providing risk-bearing capital can be changed into a Labour-Capital Partnership by admitting 'partners' who provide risk-bearing work. A Labour-Managed Cooperative can be changed into a Labour-Capital Partnership by admitting 'partners' who provide risk-bearing capital funds.

Modified Forms of Labour-Capital Partnerships

In Agathotopia there are not many cases in which the partnership principle has been applied in the undiluted form which has just been described. Thus a partnership may well need to be free to borrow some capital funds on fixed-interest contracts with the creditors (e.g. bank loans, debentures etc). On the labour side the partnership may well desire to be free to hire some forms of labour—temporary or part-time workers or consultants, for example—on fixed-wage contracts. There are also some Labour-Capital Partnerships requiring all new workers to start on a fixed-wage basis and only later offering them the option of converting a part or the whole of their pay into dividends on Labour Share Certificates.

Even more importantly some existing workers prefer to remain on fixed-wage contracts and, indeed, in some cases all the workers desire, as an insured fall-back in the case of the firm's poor performance, to remain for part of their reward on fixed-wage contracts and only for the remaining part of their reward on participation in a share of the firm's net revenue.

All of these various mixes between fixed payments and share dividends in the case both of capitalists and workers, can be incorporated in the structure of a Labour-Capital Partnership. We may define a firm's 'distributable surplus' as the value of its net revenue less expenditure on fixed interest, fixed rents, and fixed wages. Capital and Labour Share Certificates can then be issued and distributed to those who have a claim on the firm's distributable surplus. The rules and activities of the partnership can then proceed on the principles already discussed for a pure undiluted Labour-Capital Partnership. All Share Certificates, whether Capital or Labour, receive the same rate of dividend; and in effect those who have a claim on the distributable surplus, whether capitalists or workers, constitute the risk-bearing entrepreneurs.

The Management of Labour-Capital Partnerships

As will be argued later, a basic advantage which can be claimed for an Agathotopian Labour-Capital Partnership is the removal of a large range of potential conflicts of interest between labour and capital in the running of the enterprise. If the Labour-Capital Partnership principle removed literally all conflicts of interest between labour shareholders and capital shareholders the management of the enterprise would be a fairly straightforward problem. The simple answer would be to arrange that all Share Certificates, whether held by worker or by capitalist shareholders, carried an entitlement not only to the same rate of dividend but also to the same voting power at shareholders' meetings. But, as we shall see later, Agathotopian experience suggests that some areas of conflict will inevitably remain, and to resolve these it might be wise for a partnership to rule that certain decisions—or indeed that all decisions—would require the agreement of representatives of both types of partner or in the case of dispute would be referred to some form of agreed arbitration. In any case it is clear that Labour-Capital Partnerships can work only in a general atmosphere of mutual trust in which the partners wish to make the partnership work and are prepared to accept some machinery for sensible compromise in any such cases of dispute.

The following arrangement has in many cases in Agathotopia provided a reasonably independent management together with a workable process for the resolution of any conflicts of interest between workers and capitalists. The capitalist shareholders and the labour shareholders each separately elect the same number of full-time members for a board of directors. These directors appoint by agreement an additional chairman with a casting vote who thus acts as an 'arbitrator' in the case of a conflict between the two sets of directors. The board appoints a general manager who is responsible for the day-to-day conduct of the business, the agreement of the board of directors being required only for major policy decisions.

The Removal of Conflicts of Interest between Labour and Capital

In a Labour-Capital Partnership all partners receive the same dividend on their share-holdings, whether they are capitalist partners or worker partners. This arrangement removes many basic causes of conflict since a decision which raises the incomes of the existing holders of Capital Share Certificates will necessarily raise the incomes of the existing holders of Labour Share Certificates. For this reason there is much improvement in incentives and in cooperative relations between labour and capital since all stand to gain by using the existing resources of the partnership in such a way as to produce the maximum possible net revenue.

There are, of course, certain forms of 'income in kind' which may be produced in a partnership with effect upon the ease and quality of work without directly affecting the capitalist partners. One obvious case of such a possible conflict of interest could be due to a decision to devote part of the firm's resources to the provision of social amenities or fringe benefits of a type (such as canteen facilities) which would be valued by the workers but which would not confer any direct benefits on the owners of the capital invested in the business. But Agathotopian experience suggests that in an otherwise harmonious partnership differences of interest of this kind do not cause serious difficulty.

In a Discriminating Labour-Capital Partnership it is not only decisions about the use of existing resources which can in the main be taken without conflict of interest; it is also true that major decisions about changes in the scale of employment or of capital investment can be taken in such a way that any action would be to the advantage of all shareholders, whether capitalists or workers, since, if a high dividend is to result, it will result for all owners and all working partners.

The managers of the partnership would be free to decide to employ an additional worker partner by offering to him or her a new issue of Labour Share Certificates which was sufficient to attract the worker to the enterprise. If the expected dividend on these shares, while sufficient to attract the worker, was nevertheless lower than the additional revenue expected to result from the work of the new partner, all existing shareholders, whether capitalists or workers, would stand to gain by the decision, since the addition to the firm's revenue available to be paid out in increased dividends on all shares of both kinds would be greater than the additional dividend payable to the new worker on the newly issued Share Certificates. Since the new worker would presumably be attracted only if there was some advantage in accepting the offer everyone would gain from such a decision.

Exactly the same considerations would be relevant for decisions to invest in more capital equipment. The purchase of a new machine could be financed by issuing and selling on the market an issue of additional Capital Share Certificates sufficient to raise the necessary funds. All existing partners, whether Capital or Labour Shareholders, would gain if the dividend payable on the new additional Capital Share Certificates was less than the addition which the new capital equipment would add to the firm's net revenue. Thus the answer to a question whether to carry out an investment plan would depend upon a judgement whether it was to the advantage or disadvantage of all persons, whether capitalists or workers, who were concerned with the firm's activities.

Plans for expansion may often involve the simultaneous investment in new capital equipment and the employment of additional labour, and this may be so not only to expand current activities but also for the improvement of the quality of the product, for diversification into new products, for greater flexibility, for improvement of managerial control systems and so on. Moreover, much of the expenditure involved may not be on physical equipment but on the work of design and development engineers, market researchers, and other specialists. The general principle, however, remains the same. If the dividends payable on the extra Labour and Capital Share Certificates needed to attract the resources required for the firm's new plans are expected to be less than the additional net revenue which will result from the firm's new plans, the development will be to the advantage of all existing shareholders, whether workers or capitalists.

Discrimination: The End of 'Equal Pay for Equal Work'

There remains, however, for consideration one most important qualification of the rosy picture so far presented. The success of a structure of competing enterprises based on this partnership principle and, in particular, the ability of such a structure to lead to the expansion of output and thus to the maintenance of a high and stable level of employment rests upon the abandonment of any strict application of the principle of 'equal pay for equal work'.

The problem arises in the following way. Consider the position of a Labour-Capital Partnership which by efficient organisation, by a wise choice of product, by the development of technical improvements, or by other means is operating successfully. The rate of dividend which it can pay on Labour Share Certificates provides worker partners with incomes markedly in excess of the incomes of similar workers who are unemployed or are occupied in less successful enterprises.

Suppose the inside earnings of these particular worker partners is 200 while the outside incomes of many comparable workers in the rest of the economy is only 100. It may well be that an additional worker would add more than 100 but less than 200—let us say 180—to the net revenue of the partnership. If the principle of equal pay for equal work were strictly applied in the sense that a newly admitted worker partner must be offered Share Certificates which would earn him or her the 200 income of existing worker partners, the admittance of the new worker partner would be to the disadvantage of all existing partners (whether workers or capitalists) since the new worker would add 180 to the revenue but would be paid 200.

On the other hand if the new working partner were offered an issue of new Labour Share Certificates which would produce an income somewhere between 100 and 180—let us say 150—everyone would gain. All existing partners whether capitalist or labour would gain since the net revenue of the partnership would be raised by 180 at the cost of paying 150 to the new worker partner, and the new worker partner would gain by receiving 150 instead of an outsider's income of 100.

Agathotopian experience has shown that it is not sufficient to rely on expansion through the setting up of new competing partnerships. The problem of organising the new capital, management and labour, the wastes involved in not expanding the old successful organisations of capital, management and labour, and the marketing difficulties encountered by newcomers in the invasion of old markets are too great to rely solely on the launch of new enterprises, though some such expansion does occur and is always welcome.

As an alternative it has been suggested[5] that outsiders should somehow or other be given the right to demand entry to any existing partnership on the same terms as those enjoyed by the existing partners. Outsiders would presumably exercise this right and thus expand existing successful partnerships until the incomes enjoyed by the worker partners had been so reduced as to offer no further inducement for further entry. The Agathotopians have rejected this solution. It could have a disastrous effect on the return on the capital invested in the enterprise since the expansion of the business until the dividend on existing Labour Share Certificates had been halved would mean that the rate of dividend on the existing Capital Share Certificates would also be cut in half. The reward for risk-bearing capital might be turned into a punishment for success. But in any case the arrangement is thought by the Agathotopians to be impracticable. It would raise too many problems of definition and judgement concerning the skills required from new entrants for particular types of job, of compatibility of old and new partners, of resentment by existing partners of the downward pressure on their dividends, and of motivation for the successful cooperative management of concerns with unwelcome newcomers.

The principle of equal pay for equal work can be formally maintained even though newly admitted worker partners receive less than the existing insiders if, as is the case in many professional partnerships, the new partner has to purchase the right to membership of the partnership. In the preceding numerical example a new worker partner had an outsider's income of 100 but could add 180 to the income of a partnership in which the existing partners were earning 200. It would be possible for the new working partner to be given the same number of Labour Share Certificates as the existing partners (equal pay for equal work) but to be charged for the right of membership a capital sum which would finance an annuity of somewhere between 20 and 100 for a period equal to the number of years during which the new partner's pay was expected to be 200 instead of the outside 100 and the partnership was expecting to receive 180 from the new partner's work. The partnership would gain so long as the annuity was more than 20 and the new partner would gain so long as it was less than 100; and in an extreme case such as this there would be a wide margin within which a bargain could be struck which allowed for much uncertainty about future prospects. If subsequently the new worker left the partnership before the agreed period was up, he or she would be repaid by the partnership a capital sum corresponding to the remaining period of the annuity.

The Agathotopians have in some cases adopted this device. They have found it practicable to do so only in those cases in which special arrangements have been made to lend the funds necessary to enable duly qualified workers to purchase membership in successful partnerships which wished to admit them on terms agreed between the worker and the partnership. Certain groups of partnerships have in fact financed a central fund out of which loans are made to individual workers for this purpose. Due repayment of these loans out of earnings in the new partnership has been strictly enforced so that the central fund has operated on a continuously revolving basis. Experiments in which particular successful partnerships have themselves lent the necessary money directly to newly admitted worker partners have not in general been successful, since the direct deduction of repayments from dividends on Labour Share Certificates has led to individual claims for relief which have soured relations within the partnership. But where the finance of the charge for membership has been provided by a totally different independent institution the arrangement has made possible some expansion of employment at 'equal pay for equal work' to the mutual benefit of all concerned.

Yet another way of preserving the principle of equal pay for equal work without suppressing the incentives for expansion by successful partnerships may be sought by capitalising all exceptional earnings by worker partners.[6] In terms of the above numerical example suppose that in a successful partnership the existing worker partners are each receiving 200 in dividends on their Labour Share Certificates whereas the suitable rate of pay which it would be appropriate to offer to newcomers is only 100. In this case one half of the Labour Share Certificates of the existing worker partners would be converted into Capital Share Certificates so that they would now each be receiving 100 in dividends on Capital Share Certificates and only 100 for their work in the form of Labour Share Certificates. If in this way all exceptional gains of income by existing worker partners in successful partnerships were converted into returns on Capital Share Certificates, the same 'rate for the job' in terms of a fixed money wage or of dividends on Labour Share Certificates could be paid to old hands and to newly admitted workers.

This solution of the problem has been tried in Agathotopia but has proved to be dangerous in those cases in which a partnership's exceptional success has proved to be only temporary. In a growing, technologically innovative and expanding economy this is likely to be a frequent occurrence. A particular enterprise may have a particularly bright idea in introducing a new product or new technique of production. It may thereby earn an exceptionally high income but only until other enterprises have learnt to compete with it. To continue the above numerical example, suppose that a partnership has been so successful as to be able to double its rate of dividend on all Share Certificates; each working partner is receiving 200 instead of a representative outsider's income of 100. Suppose that the special earnings of the worker partners had not been capitalised. If then the special features leading to its special success disappeared, the dividend would have to be halved and the income of each working partner would revert to the outside representative market rate of 100, all earned on their Labour Share Certificates.

But if the special earnings of 100 had been converted into dividends on Capital Share Certificates, the income of each worker partner would revert to 100, but of this only 50 would be received in the form of dividends on Labour Share Certificates, the other 50 accruing in the form of dividends on Capital Share Certificates. It is a basic feature of Capital Share Certificates that such shareholdings are not tied to particular individual workers, that they can be held independently of holding a job in the partnership, and that they can be freely sold, given away, or bequeathed to the holder's heirs. In the case illustrated above worker partners with only 50 income in dividends on Labour Share Certificates would have every incentive to leave the partnership, take jobs at 100 in outside employment, and carry with them the income of 50 payable on their holding of Capital Share Certificates in the previous partnership—if they had not already disposed of them.

To retain or to replace their services their Labour Share Certificates would have to be doubled in order to restore their earned income to 100. The net result would be a dilution of the existing original capitalists' income by the issue of the additional Capital Share Certificates to capitalise the worker partners' share of what turned out to be temporary gains. The additional risks thereby imposed on those providing risk capital may be considered unacceptable.

A modified arrangement on these lines can be devised whereby from time to time any exceptional income earned by worker partners is converted from dividends on Labour Share Certificates into dividends on what can be called Bonus Share Certificates. These latter certificates would be tied like ordinary Labour Share Certificates to the individual worker partner concerned for his or her enjoyment so long as he or she was available for work in the partnership, but they would be reconvertible back into ordinary Labour Share Certificates if a reversal in the fortunes of the partnership required this in order to raise the income of existing worker partners from dividends on Labour Share Certificates up to the level of the agreed 'rate for the job'. Such a device would work simply by varying the definition of income as between 'bonus' and 'rate for the job' in such a way as to say that all worker partners, new and old, were earning the same 'rate for the job', although some were earning additional 'bonuses' in return for the special productivity achieved in the past history of the partnership. The device in no way alters the basic discrimination in pay as between old and new worker partners occupied on the same job in a partnership with a past history of special success; but it has been found in Agathotopia to be psychologically helpful in making discrimination acceptable.

The introduction of some such form of discrimination between the pay of old-established and newly admited partners in successful Labour-Capital Partnerships is essential if the system is to succeed. But Agathotopian experience also suggests that the system has some other equalising effects upon the incomes of workers. Successful Discriminating Labour-Capital Partnerships aggressively seek expansion by sucking in unemployed and low paid workers at improved incomes and this reduces inequalities between those employed in successful concerns and those who would otherwise be unemployed or earning their living in low-paid unsuccessful concerns. Thus while the system introduces an element of disparity between individual earnings within a partnership it reduces disparities of earnings between different groups of workers.

The Effect of Discriminating Labour-Capital Partnerships on the Distribution of Income between Labour and Capital

The system of Labour-Capital Partnerships is not primarily designed in itself to exert any substantial influence one way or the other in the basic distribution of income between labour and capital. However, the organisation of Labour-Capital Partnerships does have some incidental but important distributional effects and it is of interest to compare them with Capitalist Companies in this respect.

In a Capitalist Company the capitalist owners provide the entrepreneurial risk capital and hire workers at the going market rate which for any given class of labour tends to be set at a uniform rate for the competing employing companies. This cost of the employed workers to the company thus tends to represent the remuneration which the workers in question could get elsewhere. In order to remain in successful business the company must also cover the cost of its use of capital resources which similarly tends to be determined by the rate of return which the resources could earn in alternative uses. The company must thus at least cover its labour and capital costs as defined in this way, these costs being determined by the play of the forces of total demand and total supply in the markets for labour and capital. A successful business may well continue making a pure profit over and above these labour and capital costs; and in a Capitalist Company this pure profit accrues as an additional return on the risk-bearing entrepreneurial capital.

It is important to distinguish between the cases in which any such pure profit is a temporary phenomenon and the cases in which it may be a long-lasting or even a permanent phenomenon. Thus it may be due to the fact that the company has devised a new product which is much valued by consumers or a new method of production which cuts costs; but if these advantages can after a time be copied by competing companies the pure profit will be a temporary phenomenon. On the other hand the advantage which leads to a pure profit (such as a particularly favourable geographic position, a particularly effective method of production, or a special quality of product) may be protected from outside competition by the economies of scale of production. A company must be of a certain size to be able to produce successfully; and there may not be room in the particular locality or in the market for the particular brand of product for the invasion of new companies working on a sufficient scale for them to be efficient competitors. Thus one can envisage a system of successful Capitalist Companies all of which are covering their labour and capitalist costs and are also enjoying some elements of pure profit in their own particular markets.

In many respects the Agathotopian system of Discriminating Labour-Capital Partnerships is similar to this system of Capitalist Companies. It is essentially a competitive system in which each partnership must cover its labour and capital costs which as before represent the remuneration of labour and the rate of return on capital funds which these factors might be able to earn in alternative occupations. As before a partnership may enjoy a temporary pure profit over and above these costs from a new method of production or a new product before effective competition develops; and as before in other cases monopolistic advantages of locality or of brand of product and so the resulting pure profit may be permanently protected to a greater or smaller degree because the size of the market is too small to enable new partnerships to operate on a sufficiently large scale to become effective competitors.

There is however one basic difference between a Capitalist Company and a Labour-Capital Partnership: in the former the capitalist owners face the entrepreneurial risks, whereas in the latter both capitalist and worker partners are entrepreneurial risk bearers. In the former capital hires labour at a predetermined rate; in the latter capital does not hire labour and labour does not hire capital. The distribution of the pure profit between labour and capital in a Labour-Capital Partnership depends upon what has happened historically in the partnership to determine the distribution of Capital Share Certificates and Labour Share Certificates.

Thus consider the initial conversion of a Capitalist Company into a Labour–Capital Partnership. This does, of course, involve a once-for-all decision about the distribution of income between labour and capital. Should the ratio of numbers of Labour Share Certificates to Capital Share Certificates be 75 : 25 or 80 : 20 or 85 : 15? A division precisely equivalent to last year's division of the net revenue between the two classes of beneficiaries might be very seriously disputed on many grounds: Did the accountant's definition of net revenue properly represent the underlying reality? Ought not labour to increase its share if it undertakes more of the risk? What are the underlying prospects for future growth in labour earnings and capital profits? Was last year a typical year? And so on.[7]

Thus at the setting up of a Labour-Capital Partnership there may be some real conflict of interest about the issues of Labour and of Capital Share Certificates. But if the partnership is to continue successfully in business the issues of Share Certificates must be such as to cover the costs of labour and of capital. The indeterminancy and the real conflict of interest must be confined within the limits set by the prospective pure profit to be earned by the business.

As has already been explained, Agathotopian Labour-Capital Partnerships operate on what they call the Rule of Cancellation, namely the rule that on retirement a worker partner surrenders for cancellation all his or her holding of Labour Share Certificates. When the retiring worker partner is replaced by a newly engaged worker partner, sufficient new Labour Share Certificates must be issued to cover the cost of the newly engaged partner. As a result there is a net reduction in the total of Labour Share Certificates equal to the number needed to cover any pure profit over and above this cost which was enjoyed by the retiring working partner. This enables the rate of dividend per Share Certificate to be raised as the partnership's distributable surplus is paid out on a smaller number of share certificates. This means that the pure profit enjoyed by the retiring member is in effect redistributed among all remaining partners whether holders of Labour or of Capital Share Certificates. As a consequence all existing worker partners, including any recent newcomers to the workforce, will enjoy their share of the surplus so long as the incomes of the 'old hands' who are retiring exceed the starting remuneration covering the cost of the 'new hands' who replace them. The 'new hands', as they gradually become 'old hands' will obtain their increasing share of pure profit.

But the existing capitalists will also receive their share of any pure profit released by the retirement of old hands; thus not the whole of the pure profit enjoyed by retiring worker partners will be transferred to other working partners. As a result any permanent pure profit enjoyed by a successful partnership will bit by bit gradually seep away from the working partners to the holders of Capital Share Certificates. This process will in general be a prolonged one, though it will be more rapid in a capital-intensive concern in which the initial ratio of Capital to Labour Share Certificates is high. But in the long run the whole of any pure profit will be enjoyed by the owners of the capital which, unlike the retiring worker partners, is not withdrawn from the partnership.

In this respect also a Discriminating Labour-Capital Partnership operating on the rule of cancellation will in the long run come to resemble a Capitalist Company in which labour is paid its cost and all the pure profit reverts to the owners of the capital funds. Moreover in the Capitalist Company it will pay the capitalists to expand the labour force so long as the workers marginal revenue product (i.e. what he or she will add to the company's net revenue) is greater than his or her cost (i.e. his or her wage): and in the Discriminating Labour-Capital Partnership under the rule of cancellation it will also in the long run pay all existing partners, both workers and capitalists, to engage an additional working partner so long as his or her marginal revenue product is greater than his or her cost. In this respect also the two systems have very similar mechanisms determining the ultimate expansion of the work force.

But there may be one very significant difference in the outcome. The cost of a worker may be much lower for the Discriminating Labour-Capital Partnership than for the Capitalist Company and thus the expansionary forces may be greater in the former than in the latter system. In a Capitalist Company existing workers (the insiders) wish through trade union action or by other means to protect their rate of pay against the possibility of new workers (the outsiders) offering their services at a lower rate. In a Discriminating Partnership the lower the remuneration of new partners, the greater the gain to the existing members who are already inside the partnership; and thus the insiders will encourage the outsiders to offer their service at the lowest rate of remuneration which is attractive to them rather than impeding them from so doing. The result would be in principle the same as that which would be achieved by a set of similar Capitalist Companies on the assumption that their fixed wage rates were set at a low enough level to give an incentive to the capitalist employers to employ all workers who sought employment at those rates. There could be some important advantages in the partnership economy due to the greater productivity resulting from improvements in incentives and the reduction of conflicts between labour and capital in the running of businesses. But in principle in the final steady state the distribution of income between labour and capital in the Discriminating Labour-Capital Partnerships would be the same as in a set of similar Capitalist Companies on the assumption that the latters' fixed wage rates were held down to the level necessary to achieve full employment.

On the other hand, the disadvantage is, of course, the possible adverse effects upon the real remuneration of the working partners and on the distribution of income between the owners of Capital Share Certificates and of Labour Share Certificates. Full employment in a free market economy, whether it be composed of Capitalist Companies or of Labour-Capital Partnerships, may imply a relatively low rate of real remuneration for the work done and thus a substantial rise in the share going to the owners of capital, a phenomenon which could become particularly marked if modern technological developments proved to be basically labour-saving. It is for this reason that the Agathotopians have always insisted that their system of Discriminating Labour-Capital Partnerships at the enterprise level should be combined with the very extensive fiscal and other measures for the redistribution of income and wealth which are described later in Part III of this tract.

But it may be questioned whether the pure profit of a partnership, whose success has been created and is maintained by risk-bearing worker partners as well as by the providers of risk-bearing capital, should all seep away to the sole benefit of the capitalist partners, as will certainly be the case under the rule of cancellation. Cannot some alternative rule for the treatment of retiring worker partners be devised which would avoid this undesirable distributive effect?

Alternative Treatments of Retiring Worker Partners

In the Agathotopian Labour-Capital Partnerships there are usually arrangements under which the retiring member obtains a pension financed out of contributions previously paid into a pension fund by the individual worker partner and by the partnership.

These contributions are payable as a stated percentage of the annual earnings of the member and thus the pension does reflect both the cost element and the pure-profit element in the retiring member's past remuneration. The arrangement thus boils down to a system of financing a working partner's retirement out of compulsory savings by the member during his or her period of service with the partnership, the contributions in fact representing a part of the income which could have been paid to the member in the absence of a pension arrangement. These pension arrangements are in no essential way different from the pension arrangements normally found in a Capitalist Company.

What may be distinctive about the treatment of a retiring worker member of a Labour-Capital Partnership is the treatment of the Labour Share Certificates held by the member on his or her retirement. In Agathotopia there has been much debate about the possibility of finding an alternative to the Rule of Cancellation, the nature and effects of which have been discussed in the previous section.

A case is made out for drawing a distinction between the retiring working partner's cost and the retiring working partner's pure profit and for dividing his or her holding of Labour Share Certificates into two parts: (i) an amount of certificates the return on which is needed to pay for the partner's cost and (ii) any remaining excess of certificates the return on which will in fact be financing the partner's pure profit. These two parts are called cost certificates and pure-profit certificates respectively.

It is universally agreed that a retiring working partner's cost certificates should be surrendered and cancelled. This is necessary in order to offset the new issue of the same amount of certificates which will be needed to attract a new partner to replace the retiring worker partner. There is, however, a certain debate about what would be the appropriate treatment of the pure-profit certificates. One group supports a so-called Rule of Retention, namely that the retiring working partner's pure-profit certificates should be retained by the retiring member after being transformed into ordinary Capital Share Certificates; another group supports a so-called Rule of Redistribution, namely that the retiring working partner's pure-profit certificates should be redistributed in equal amounts of Labour Share Certificates among all the remaining worker partners.

In brief in all cases a retiring working partner's cost certificates would be cancelled and thus make room for their reissue to a new partner to replace the retiring partner. The debate concerns only the treatment of pure-profit certificates which would also be cancelled under the rule of cancellation, retained by the retiring partner in the form of Capital Share Certificates under the rule of retention, and redistributed in the form of Labour Share Certificates among the remaining worker partners under the rule of redistribution.

The choice between these three modes of treating a retiring worker partner's pure-profit certificates can have important distributive effects. Consider first the case of a partnership which is enjoying a permanent and lasting element of pure profit. Initially when the partnership is first set up or when the pure profit is first experienced it is shared between labour and capital in the form of a high rate of dividend on Labour Share Certificates and Capital Share Certificates.

With the rule of redistribution there is no change in the distribution of pure profit as between capital and labour. As the years go by the pure profit of any retiring worker partner is simply handed back to the remaining worker partners.

With the rules of cancellation and of retention as the years go by the pure profit enjoyed by worker partners is reduced and that enjoyed by capitalist partners is increased by the same amount until in the end in both cases the original worker's pure profit has all been transferred to the enjoyment of the capitalists. But there are three important distinctions between the two cases.

First, the mechanisms of transfer are very different in the two cases. With the rule of cancellation, as was explained in the previous section, the mechanism works simply through cancellation of retiring worker partners' pure-profit certificates which allows the rate of dividend on the remaining total of Share Certificates to rise, thus enriching the original providers of capital funds. With the rule of retention the mechanism works simply by transforming the pure-profit certificates of retiring worker partners into Capital Share Certificates without any change in the total number of certificates issued.

Second, this leads to a difference in the distribution of pure-profit among the owners of Capital Share Certificates. With the rule of cancellation the original capitalists obtain the whole of the advantage; with the rule of retention a new class of capitalist obtains the whole of the advantage, leaving the original capitalists' pure profit unchanged.

Third, the process of transfer is much more rapid with the rule of retention than with the rule of cancellation. With the former the whole of a retiring worker's pure profit is immediately transformed into a capitalist pure profit; with the rule of cancellation at each retirement only a fraction of the working partner's pure profit is transferred to the capitalists, a proportion which may be very low in a labour-intensive partnership.

From the distributional point of view one may prefer the rule of redistribution, which in fact retains pure profit for working partners and one may consider the rule of cancellation to be the least desirable since it ultimately transfers all pure profit to the original providers of the risk capital. The rule of retention by creating new owners of capital out of retiring worker partners may have some indirect distributive merit in that it may lead to a wider spread of the ownership of capital.

There is, however, a quite different danger which may arise from the application of the rule of redistribution. The principle of discrimination is advocated in Agathotopia on the grounds that it will lead to an expansion in the number of working partners so long as an additional working partner would add more to the partnership's revenue than the cost to the partnership of the new working partner.

But consider the attitude of some young working partners who have recently been engaged in a highly profitable partnership, working under the rule of redistribution. They will expect a rise in their remuneration as older partners retire and their pure profit is redistributed. It will be to the advantage of the younger partners that the engagement of new partners should be restricted so that there should be a smaller number of potential beneficiaries in the future redistributions of pure profit—an advantage which will disappear only if the number of working partners is so restricted that the potential addition to the total revenue of the partnership due to an expansion of the number of working partners is so large as to offset the redistributive loss.

The possible gain from restriction of membership will be greater for the younger partners than for the older partners on the point of retirement who have little to gain from future redistribution. It will be increased (i) if the amount of pure profit enjoyed by the partnership is large, (ii) if the partnership is a labour-intensive one so that little of the pure profit is enjoyed by the owners of Capital Share Certificates and (iii) if the rate at which younger partners discount the value of future benefits is low.

If the partnership operates under the rule of cancellation, the prospective redistributive gains for the younger members will from the outset be weakened because the pure profit of retiring worker partners will have to be shared by the capitalist members; and this weakening of the motive for restriction will be greater, the more capital-intensive is the partnership. Moreover as the years go by the motive for restriction will become smaller and smaller as the labour pure profit seeps away to the capitalists until in the end there is no labour pure profit left to be redistributed and thus no motive for restriction.

The motive for restriction will from the outset be non-existent under the rule of retention since newly engaged workers will have no prospect of any redistributive gain and thus no incentive to reduce the numbers eligible to share in the gain.[8]

Thus the rule of retention has the great advantage of not weakening the expansionist force of the principle of discrimination. But if a partnership's enjoyment of a pure profit turns out to be only temporary the rule of retention carries with it the danger of another kind from which the rules of redistribution and of cancellation are immune. Consider a partnership (i) which starts with no pure profit with Capital Share Certificates and Labour Share Certificates issued in amounts which just cover the costs of capital and labour (ii) which then passes through a lucky period with a high demand for its product and with worker and capitalist partners enjoying a pure profit *pro rata* on their share holdings, and (iii) which after a considerable period loses its market advantage and reverts to its original position just covering its costs. With the rule of redistribution this presents no special problems; during the lucky period even with a complete turnover of the working partnership, the working partners will enjoy the pure profit while it lasts and will just cover their costs when the lucky period is over.

The mechanism is different with the rule of cancellation but the final result is the same. During the lucky period the high pure profit will all seep away to the capitalist members of the partnership, the remuneration of the worker partners reverting to the level of their costs as new working partners are engaged on the discriminating principles. As we have seen this transfer of the pure profit will be brought about by a rise in the rate of dividend on a diminishing total of Share Certificates. When the pure profit disappears the consequential reduction in the rate of dividend will mean that the new set of working partners will no longer cover their costs. In order to retain their services the partnership will have to issue additional Labour Share Certificates to them. But when they have received a new issue of Labour Share Certificates equal to the amount of labour pure-profit certificates which had been cancelled as working partners retired during the high-profit period, the situation will once more revert to its original position with worker and capitalist partners both just covering their costs.

The situation is, however, basically different with the rule of retention. In this case during the period of high profit retiring worker partners' pure-profit certificates will gradually be transformed into Capital Share Certificates held by retired working partners or dispersed among their heirs or among other persons to whom these Capital Share Certificates have been sold. When the high profit disappears the costs of the existing worker partners will no longer be covered unless they receive an issue of additional Labour Share Certificates to make up for the loss of such certificates due to their transformation into the Capital Share Certificates issued to retired worker partners; the result is a net increase in the total of Capital Share Certificates with a restoration of the issue of Labour Share Certificates to its original position before the high-profit period. The increased issue of Capital Share Certificates will merely dilute the return to those who originally supplied the capital funds. There would be a strong disincentive against investing capital funds in a risky enterprise with the prospect of fluctuating fortunes. Those who subscribed such risk capital would be confronted with a situation in which they shared any profit with working partners but must face the whole of any subsequent loss of such profits insofar as the labour share of the profit had meanwhile been capitalised on the retirement of working partners. This argument against the rule of retention is thus a modified form of the argument expressed earlier (in the discussion of the principle of equal pay for equal work) against the immediate capitalisation of all labour pure profit.

In Agathotopia the normal arrangement is to operate a Discriminating Labour-Capital Partnership under the rule of cancellation. This choice is due partly to its being recognised as a compromise between the advantages and the dangers of both the principles of redistribution and of retention. It avoids the danger which retention carries with it of extreme dilution of the interest of existing capitalist partners; it leads to a prolonged period during which much pure profit is redistributed to worker partners, but it avoids going to the extreme form of redistribution with its possible serious adverse restrictive effects on the size of the working membership; indeed with the rule of cancellation any such restrictive influence diminishes progressively to vanishing point as labour pure profit seeps away to the capitalist partners. But there is in the opinion of the Agathotopians a second very powerful argument in favour of the rule of cancellation, namely its simplicity. The other rules both rely upon distinguishing between a retiring working partner's pure profit and his or her cost, thus necessitating an assessment of what would in effect be the replacement cost of the particular worker. The simple rule of cancellation of all the partner's Labour Share Certificates avoids this difficult and very contentious issue.

The Renegotiation of Share Holdings

The main negotiation of the distribution of share holdings between capitalist and worker partners must take place on the inauguration of the partnership. But some subsequent occasions will occur when a renegotiation of share certificates issued to existing worker partners or capitalist partners is needed. Individual promotions are, of course, a proper and desirable phenomenon— indeed, a necessary one if able persons are to be retained in the partnership's service. In such cases promotions involving the raising of a worker's pay by a rise in his or her fixed-wage payment or by the issue to him or her of additional Labour Share Certificates are, of course, of ultimate benefit to all shareholders.

But the problem becomes much more serious if one considers the possibility of group claims for 'promotion', i.e. for renegotiation of the number of Labour Share Certificates issued to a whole class of workers. Suppose there were a threat of a strike by all the worker partners in a particular enterprise unless the ratio of Labour Share Certificates to Capital Share Certificates were radically altered. Or suppose that a particular small group of worker partners who were in a key position to hold up operations threatened to strike unless their claim to an increased issue of Share Certificates was satisfied.

Such a claim might, of course, be justified if outside developments had so increased their value that they would be tempted to move elsewhere unless their claim was met. The Agathotopians have found that in every partnership there must be some agreed arrangement whereby claims for 'promotion' can be made by individuals or groups of partners on the grounds that new improved terms of payment which they are claiming are (i) necessary to offset the attraction of employment in other outside concerns and (ii) do not exceed the loss of net revenue to the partnership which would occur if they withdraw their services. It is an essential part of the agreed machinery of a Labour-Capital Partnership that such claims are submitted to some appropriate organ of the partnership for decision and that this implies the end of partnership membership for those who do not accept the award.

The Treatment of Undistributed Revenue

There is one further important class of events which may give rise to the need for a new additional issue of Share Certificates to existing partners. This need could arise from the fact that Labour Share Certificates give entitlement to a dividend only until retirement age, while Capital Share Certificates give an entitlement to a dividend for the indefinite future. A worker partner, particularly if he or she is near retiring age, is naturally less concerned than is a holder of Capital Share Certificates with the effect of management decisions on the future fortunes of the partnership and is more concerned with their more immediate present effects.

Such a conflict of interest could be wholly avoided if it were possible always to adopt an accounting procedure which would give a clear and unequivocal definition of what was the partnership's distributable surplus in any period, in the sense of the amount of dividends that could be distributed to the shareholders and yet leave enough funds to ensure that the real capital resources of the partnership were so maintained as to allow this same level of real distributable surplus to be sustained indefinitely in the future. If less were distributed, then capital resources would be more than maintained so that some part of current distributable surplus should be treated as a net saving. If more were distributed in dividends, then the partnership would be dissaving and living on its capital to that extent.

In these conditions an appropriate arrangement would be that there should be an issue of additional Capital Share Certificates equal at current valuations to the amount of distributable surplus which was not distributed in dividend, and that these additional Capital Share Certificates instead of being sold in the market should be distributed in lieu of dividend *pro rata* to all existing share holders whether workers or capitalists. Thus workers as well as capitalists would acquire Capital Share Certificates (which they would be perfectly free to hold or to sell as they chose), to represent that part of the partnership's income which had been held back from distribution on their existing share certificates. Alternatively it would be possible to arrange for the dividend on Capital Share Certificates to be cut without cutting the dividend on Labour Share Certificates and to issue the additional Capital Share Certificates solely to the existing holders of such certificates, so that it was only the capitalists who financed and who benefited from the ploughing back of revenue into an expansion of the capital resources of the business.

There is one further tiresome complication which has to be introduced into the accounting procedure of a Labour-Capital Partnership. For worker partners who rely for a main part of their income on Labour Share Certificates it is necessary to pay such dividends at frequent intervals, possibly even weekly, and at rates which are reasonably stable and reliable. Any such distribution involves some administrative costs and accounting problems, even though dividends on Capital Share Certificates can continue to be paid yearly or half-yearly. But more importantly rates of dividend have to be announced some time in advance of payment so that worker partners have some knowledge of the incomes on which they can rely at least for a number of months in advance. This involves for accounting purposes some kind of dividend equalisation fund into which distributable surplus can be paid subject to inevitable variation between good and bad periods and from which more stable, reliable and frequent dividends could be paid.

Such accounting arrangements inevitably complicate somewhat the distinctions to be drawn between capital and current payments and receipts. But the problem in fact goes much deeper in trying to make a fair calculation of the probable level at which real distributable surplus could be sustained. Quite apart from problems which arise as a result of monetary inflation, the problems are especially great in cases where future risks and uncertainty are important. Suppose that the management of a partnership were confronted with the possibility of replacing part of its capital equipment with equipment based on a new technology which would admittedly not produce a very high return in the near future period of inevitable teething troubles but which might, if successful, produce an exceedingly high return in future years. The holders of Labour Share Certificates—and in particular those nearing retiring age—would have every justification in demanding that an accounting procedure should be adopted which treated the low returns expected during the immediate low years as due to savings which were being made in order to lead to the uncertain, but hoped-for, high returns of the later years. But quite what allowances should be made for the uncertainty surrounding these venturesome new technologies and what rates of discount should be used to evaluate them in order to make the relevant calculations are matters for somewhat arbitrary choice.

The Agathotopians make every effort to apply the principle that in the case of undistributed net revenue new Capital Share Certificates should be issued to those, whether capitalist or worker partners, who have been deprived of the distribution. But they recognise the difficulties in applying this principle and regard its application as contributing one of the most important reasons for ensuring that every partnership has an agreed arrangement for seeking appropriate impartial arbitration in case of potential conflict of opinion on issues of this kind.

The Treatment of Capital Gains

The need to issue new Capital Share Certificates to workers arises in those cases in which less has been distributed in dividends than the distributable surplus which could be sustained indefinitely with the existing equipment of men and machines. This does not imply that any such distribution of Capital Share Certificates to worker partners should be made whenever the capital shareholders enjoy a capital gain.

Consider a case in which (for example, because of a once-for-all increase in the demand for the product of the partnership) the value of the net revenue which can be indefinitely produced by an unchanged equipment of men and machines rises by 10 per cent in value. A 10 per cent increase in all dividend payments on Capital and Labour Share Certificates can be made. The market value of the Capital Share Certificates as well as the income on such Share Certificates will have risen by 10 per cent. But so also will the income on Labour Share Certificates have risen by 10 per cent, so that the present discounted capital value of any individual worker partner's future income from his Labour Share Certificates will also have risen by 10 per cent. There has been no holding back of sustainable income from distribution to worker partners in order to increase the concern's capital equipment so as to produce a higher sustainable output. There has been an exogenous change which has increased the value of the output sustainable by an unchanged equipment of men and machines; and this has increased the present discounted value of

Capital Share Certificates and of Labour Share Certificates by 10 per cent in both cases.

The Effect of Security of Tenure for Worker Partners

In a Discriminating Labour-Capital Partnership a worker partner who became redundant would retain his or her income from Labour Share Certificates until the age of retirement so long as he or she was available for work in the partnership. In a Capitalist Company the worker would have no such security of tenure. The question arises whether this arrangement unduly shifts the distribution of income against the capitalist partners since redundant worker partners retain an income which in the case of a Capitalist Company would revert to the owners of the capital.

There is a very important offsetting advantage for the capitalist partners. If there is a reduction in the demand for the partnership's product which leads to a reduction in the enterprise's distributable surplus, the dividends on Labour Share Certificates will be reduced *pari passu* with the dividends in Capital Share Certificates. The reduction in the incomes of the capitalist partners is in large part offset by the reduction in the incomes of the worker partners. What in a Capitalist Company employing workers at a fixed rate of pay would lead to redundancy will lead to a reduction in labour costs in a Labour-Capital Partnership. In general those who provide risk capital to a Labour-Capital Partnership are likely to gain more by being able to retain worker partners who share the loss with them than they will lose by the risk of having to support them if they become redundant.

But there are certain other kinds of event which may lead to redundancies for which the security of tenure in a Labour-Capital Partnership does impose a burden on the return to be earned on risk-bearing capital which would be avoided in a Capitalist Company. This could arise in the case of what would otherwise be a profitable introduction of certain new technologies. The replacement of existing workers by a machine or by workers of a different skill would be profitable in a Capitalist Company if the wages payable to the existing workers were greater than the current costs of the new machine or of the new team of workers; such a replacement could be held up in a partnership in which the dismissal of an existing worker would, up to retirement age, save only the fixed-wage element but not the share-dividend element in the worker partner's remuneration. Any such delay would be mitigated in three ways: first it would operate only in so far as it would otherwise be desirable to introduce the new technology more rapidly than could be covered by the normal ageing and retirement of the workforce; second, the extra cost of replacement of an existing worker would refer only to that part of his or her pay which took the form of a dividend on Labour Share Certificates; and, third, it would be wholly avoided by any new firm which was set up to exploit the new technology. Moreover, the net loss arising from any such impediments to the introduction of new technologies should not be exaggerated. There are already in normal Capitalist Companies some serious impediments on account of trade union and similar pressure to preserve existing jobs and demarcations of work and on account of statutory or other obligations to make redundancy payments to redundant workers.

The cost to a partnership involved in the support of redundant worker partners is also limited by the principle stated above that the claim of a worker partner on the partnership would be tied to his or her availability to perform the work for which the dividend on Labour Share Certificates was the reward. An 'availability' test might be applied by ruling that a partnership which made a worker partner redundant could at any time ask the worker to return to the partnership on the terms which he or she previously enjoyed with it. If the worker concerned declined the invitation, then his or her Labour Share Certificates would be cancelled. The existence of this rule would ensure that redundant workers who did subsequently find an alternative post which held out more attractive prospects of future work could be effectively asked once and for all to surrender their existing Labour Share Certificates.

The application of this simple 'availability' test does, however, raise an important and far-reaching problem. In the case of a worker partner the whole of whose pay consisted of dividends on Labour Share Certificates, there would be no problem in defining 'the terms which he or she had previously enjoyed' with the partnership. The worker would be offered a post with the retention of an unchanged number of Labour Share Certificates. But in the case of workers who had received a fixed-wage element in their previous pay in the partnership, the problem would arise as to what level of fixed pay they should be offered on reinstatement. The same money rate of pay might well be unfair if, for example, inflationary developments during the period of absence from the partnership had substantially eroded the value of money. Since the partnership is founded on the principle that fixed-money wages are not intended to represent the whole of, or indeed any specific proportion of, the real pay of any individual worker, there would be no obvious 'rate for the job' on which to base the new offer. It would be necessary to rely on some rather general definition such as 'the rate which the worker could reasonably be expected to be receiving if he or she had continued an unbroken membership of the partnership', backed by some form of arbitration or review by an independent tribunal in the case of disagreement.

There is one further source of trouble which may arise in the treatment of redundancy. It is proposed that worker partners who leave the enterprise voluntarily to seek better paid jobs should surrender their Labour Share Certificates, whereas a worker partner who is made redundant should at least for the time being retain them. It would thus be to the interest of workers who wished to move elsewhere to be judged redundant rather than themselves to resign their membership of the partnership. For this purpose they might make themselves as useless as possible to the management without stepping over the borderline which would justify dismissal for misconduct with consequential surrender of their Labour Share Certificates. The conflict of interest in this case would be between the delinquent worker partners on the one hand and all other partners, whether worker or capitalist, on the other hand; but there is clearly here the possibility of tiresome disputes requiring judgement by some form of impartial tribunal. This particular problem would, however, be greatly eased if the test of availability proposed above were adopted, since a worker who obtained a more attractive job and who retained the Labour Share Certificates issued by the partnership in which he or she previously worked could always be induced to surrender them by being invited to rejoin the partnership on the original but now unattractive terms of service.

The Implication for Risk Bearing

There is a very good reason why the owners of the equity capital rather than the workers should bear the risks of fluctuations in the profitability of any enterprise. Owners of capital can spread their risks by investing their capital in relatively small amounts in a large number of independent enterprises. If one enterprise fares very badly, they will not have all their eggs in one basket. It is impossible for a worker to split up his or her working hours into small periods of an hour a week and thus work one hour each week for, say, 40 different firms. Work eggs unlike capital eggs must all be held in one basket, or at the most in one or two baskets.

But any form of partnership enterprise in which the incomes of the worker partners depend in whole or part upon the fortunes of the enterprise necess-arily implies that the workers face risks which they would not otherwise confront. In this way they share with the capitalists risks which would other-wise have been borne wholly by the capitalists. If the concern does well the capitalists share the gain with the workers; if it does badly the workers share the loss by receiving a lower rate of reward. In this way the capitalists face smaller risks and the workers greater risks of variation in their incomes.

There is thus a basic dilemma between the objective of concentrating risk-bearing on those who provide the capital funds and the objective of treating workers as full partners in a business enterprise. Certain forms of partnership enterprise accentuate this dilemma by requiring or at least encouraging wor-kers to own capital shares in the enterprise in which they work and thus to become directly concerned with its profitability. But this increases the concentration of risks borne by the workers since it ensures that not only their work eggs but also a part at least of their capital eggs are in one and the same basket.

Agathotopian Discriminating Labour-Capital Partnerships avoid this anomaly. Measures are taken in Agathotopia (as described later in Part III of this tract) to encourage a widespread ownership of capital funds so that the representative worker partner does own capital funds to invest in the Capital Share Certificates of Labour-Capital Partnerships. But there is no call on a worker partner to invest in the Capital Share Certificates of the particular partnership in which he or she works. On the contrary like good capitalists worker partners are encouraged to spread their capital risks over a wide range of other partnerships.

But even if this form of unnecessary concentration of capital risks is avoided, the basic dilemma regarding the risks to which earned incomes are subject in Labour-Capital Partnerships remains unsolved and gives rise to the following questions.

(1) Should partnership enterprises be encouraged in order to promote better incentives and better relations between labour and capital and, in their discriminating form, to promote full employment? Or should they be discouraged in order to enable risks to be concentrated on the owners of capital?

(2) Whatever answer be given to the first question, a second question arises. Can workers be persuaded to become risk-bearing partners rather than employees at fixed rates of pay or must Labour-Capital Partnerships be dismissed as an unacceptable pipe dream?

(3) If Labour-Capital Partnerships are in fact constructed with the worker partners playing an effective role in their management, will there not be a dangerous bias introduced against risky business, a bias which could seriously impede economic innovation and progress?

These considerations suggest that to enable a successful and acceptable structure of Labour-Capital Partnerships to be developed it will be necessary to introduce some measures to mitigate the risk problem for the worker partners. Such measures are discussed later in Part III of this tract.

This problem of risk-bearing should not, however be exaggerated. There are certain aspects of partnership enterprises which reduce the risks of workers. In particular a worker partner faces a smaller risk of unemployment than does an employee engaged at a fixed rate of pay. Thus while the worker partner stands to gain in income if the enterprise does well, he or she has less fear of his or her income falling to the level of unemployment benefit if the enterprise does badly. It is the capitalist and those workers who are most likely to become unemployed who face less risk in a Labour-Capital Partnership. It is the workers whose jobs are secure who face the greater risks in the fluctuations of their dividend income. Can workers then be free to choose between employment at a fixed wage rate and partnership with a variable dividend?

In a Labour-Capital Partnership the existing capitalist and worker partners would have an incentive to make a fellow worker partner redundant only if they judged that what he or she contributed to the firm's net revenue had fallen below the amount of the fixed-wage element in his or her pay, since any dividends payable on Labour Share Certificates would remain a charge on the partnership's income, whether the worker partner was made redundant or not. Thus a worker by choosing any given mix between a fixed-wage payment and a dividend on Labour Share Certificates would thereby in effect have chosen to distribute risks in a corresponding mix between unemployment and fluctuations in the inclusive rate of remuneration. The higher the fixed-wage element, the greater the risk of unemployment but the lower the risk of a drop—or indeed of a rise—in his or her inclusive rate of remuneration.

In many businesses the existing workers may have a pretty shrewd idea as to which of them are regarded as least productive by the management and are, therefore, the most likely to be made redundant if a reduction in the labour force becomes necessary. Thus a known minority of workers may face an important risk of unemployment which does not threaten the majority. In such a case if the mix between a fixed wage and a share dividend had to apply equally to all workers, the choice of the majority would be for a fixed wage. If, however, it were possible for individual workers to make their own choice, those most liable to redundancy might well choose a variable dividend. Such a choice would give them relative security of employment; the next layer of relatively unproductive workers would now be those who risked redundancy and would thus become more favourable to the variable dividend, and so on by a domino effect the total mix would contain a larger and larger proportion of variable dividend.

In a number of Agathotopian partnerships workers have been allowed freely to choose (on terms laid down by the management of the partnership) between fixed-wage payments and receipts of dividends on Labour Share Certificates, but their experience has suggested that while the resulting domino effect does something to help it cannot be relied upon alone to persuade the representative worker to accept a very substantial proportion of pay in the form of a variable dividend.

In addition to the lower risks of unemployment in a Labour-Capital Partnership there is a second factor which mitigates the risk to workers. In a Labour-Capital Partnership worker partners remain free to move to other occupations. To the extent to which this factor is operative, the worker is presented with a heads-I-win-tails-you-lose situation. If the enterprise does well the worker partner shares the gain with the capitalist partner; if the enterprise does badly the worker partner avoids the loss by moving elsewhere, leaving the capitalist partner to bear the risk in the same way as he would have done in a Capitalist Company. In reality the worker partner will normally not be able to avoid all risk in this way. If the bad fortune of the partnership is part of the phenomenon of a general depression, there will not be any attractive alternative occupations to move to. Even if the bad fortune is peculiar to the partnership, the availability of alternative occupations will depend upon the particular conditions of the region and the occupation in which the trouble has arisen; and in any case the search for and shift to the alternative occupation will be costly and will take time. But there may be cases in which the possibility of voluntary movement to alternative jobs significantly shifts risks back again from the worker on to the capitalist.

There are many other factors which affect the degree of risk borne by worker partners and by capitalist partners in a Labour-Capital Partnership. The preceding discussion has been confined to a comparison between a Capitalist Company and a Labour-Capital Partnership. If however, the relevant transformation had been that of a Labour-Managed Cooperative into a Labour-Capital Partnership, the changes to risk bearing would have been totally different. Moreover, the nature and degree of change will depend upon many other factors: whether the enterprise is in a capital-intensive or a labour-intensive activity; whether the risk to be borne is on the supply side (e.g. a risk concerning future techniques of production) or, as has been assumed throughout the above analysis, on the demand side; whether the change is expected to be permanent or temporary; whether it is expected to occur soon or only in the distant future; whether the change is general to a whole region or industry or occupation or whether it is confined to a single particular partnership; and so on.

It is impossible to cover all these possibilities. But Agathotopian experience suggests that it can be safely concluded that for the successful introduction of Discriminating Labour-Capital Partnerships as a major, if not the predominant, form for competitive private enterprise, it will be necessary to take some special measures to mitigate the risks borne by worker partners.

Conclusions

From the above discussion of the nature of partnership enterprises the following conclusions may be reached:

(i)   that they could lead to a great encouragement of cooperative action between labour and capital in running a competitive concern in the most efficient and productive manner; and

(ii) that they could lead to an expansion of an enterprise's workforce and thus to a reduction in unemployment, if the obstacle presented by a strict application of the principle of equal pay for equal work were overcome; but

(iii) that they cannot be expected in themselves to lead to any basic improvement in the distribution of income between labour and capital; and

(iv) that their acceptance by workers may be seriously impeded by their implications as regards the bearing of risks.

In the following Part III on The Partnership Economy an attempt is made to see how far Agathotopian experience suggests that general economic and financial institutions and policies may be moulded so as to reduce the obstacles to the widespread acceptance of partnership at the enterprise level.

Part III The Partnership Economy

The conclusions reached at the end of Part II suggest that a successful and acceptable development of partnership enterprises depends upon three conditions: (1) the erosion of the principle of equal pay for equal work, (2) the design of other measures for the improvement of the distribution of income and wealth, and (3) the alleviation of the risks to be borne by worker partners. Thus the structure of a system of partnership enterprises needs to be undertaken against the background of a partnership economy in which general economic policies and institutions are designed to meet these three requirements. The present Part III of this tract is accordingly devoted to an analysis of the special features which in these respects distinguish the Agathotopian economy from that with which we are familiar in the United Kingdom.

The Distribution of Income and Wealth

As has been argued in Part II, Labour-Capital Partnerships must not be relied upon as an instrument for achieving any desired change in the distribution of the product of industry as between the incomes of workers and of owners of capital. But what is really important is not the distribution of the national income between labour as a whole and capital as a whole, but the distribution of income between individuals. It is no doubt true that the common contrast between very rich capitalists on the one hand and very poor workers on the other has rather more reality than a contrived contrast between very poor capitalists (the proverbial widows and orphans) on the one hand and very rich workers (the great operatic singer or the computer expert) on the other. But the way to cope with the problem is to devise ways of influencing the distribution of income between rich and poor persons rather than to upset efficient working of the competitive market economy by direct control of the division between the return on capital and the earnings of labour.

What then are the general policies which might be adopted in a partnership economy to deal with this problem of distribution? Such measures can be summarised under four broad headings.

First, there are measures designed to encourage a more equal distribution of the ownership of property. If the representative citizen were both a rep-

28

resentative worker and a representative capitalist providing the national average amount of work per head and owning the national average amount of capital per head, a market change which caused a larger proportion of the national product to go to capital and less to labour would have no effect on his or her individual income. What the citizen lost in payment for labour he or she would gain in payment on wealth. A widespread ownership of property is a most desirable feature of a partnership economy. Not only would it help to deal with the basic problem of the distribution of income between individuals. It would also at the partnership enterprise level help to promote the atmosphere of cooperative partnership if every worker owner of Labour Share Certificates also owned an appreciable amount of Capital Share Certificates, even if those were invested in other partnerships.

A second method for equalising the income accruing from the ownership of property is for the State itself to become the beneficial owner of a part of the country's income-generating capital resources and to use the income earned on this capital wealth to finance the payment of a Social Dividend to all citizens. This method involves the State in acquiring through its fiscal policy a Net National Asset to replace the customary present Net National Debt. Both methods have the effect of distributing to the private citizens the income earned on capital wealth on a more equal basis. These methods become the more significant, the greater is the proportion of the national product which in a free market economy would accrue to capital rather than the labour. It may well be true that in a competitive market economy the achievement and maintenance of full employment in the UK demands some reduction in the real cost of the worker's remuneration and thus some shift to profit, a development which would become even more important if future technological changes turned out to be markedly labour-saving in the sense that they markedly increased the importance of capital equipment relative to manpower in the processes of production.

Third, there is the possibility of the State providing on the same equal basis for all citizens certain social services such as those for education and health.

Fourth, there is the possibility of direct redistribution of money incomes between rich and poor through the payment of direct monetary social benefits in support of the poor financed by some form of progressive taxation of the rich.

In Agathotopia, as will be explained later, special measures have been devised to encourage a more widespread ownership of property and to exert a direct equalising effect upon the distribution of income.

Risk-Bearing

In Part II the question was raised whether the development of Labour-Capital Partnerships might be impeded by the unwillingness of workers to bear the risks of a form of pay which varied with the fortunes of the business in which they were employed.

The more equal distribution of the ownership of property which is one of the features of the Agathotopian economy has helped to deal with this problem. The greater the proportion of income which a worker receives from property which can be invested in other undertakings, the more ready he or she will be to face possible fluctuations in his or her remuneration for work.

A second feature of the same kind is the payment by the State to every citizen (dependent solely upon the age and family position of that citizen) of a given income, called a Social Dividend. This income is tax-free and is paid unconditionally to every citizen whether he or she is employed or unemployed, healthy or sick, active or idle, and—at the appropriate rates—young or old. The representative citizen then has four sources of income.

(i)   a certain and reliable tax free Social Dividend,

(ii) the return on his or her capital wealth which he or she can lend at fixed interest or at a probably higher yield in equity capital, the risks of which can be spread over a large number of enterprises,

(iii) any part of his or her remuneration for work which continues to take the form of a fixed wage payment, and

(iv) the whole or the part of the remuneration for his or her work which takes the form of a share in the fluctuating revenue of the partnership in which the work is done.

Items (i), (ii) and (iii) mitigate the risks involved in (iv).

Full Employment and the Flexibility of Pay for Work

Full employment implies a level of employment which is both stable and high. It is the flexibility of rates of pay in Discriminating Labour-Capital Partnerships which in Agathotopia leads to a satisfactory employment situation. A stable level is achieved in so far as remuneration for work takes the form of a variable dividend on Labour Share Certificates instead of a fixed wage rate. If demand for the products of the enterprise falls off, the rate of dividend on both Capital and Labour Share Certificates is reduced; production costs and prices are lowered; employment and output are maintained at lower money costs and prices rather than being reduced in volume at unchanged money prices. But a high level of employment is achieved not through the variability of the pay of existing workers but through the principle of discrimination which gives an incentive to existing partners to mop up any pockets of involuntarily unemployed persons at rates of remuneration which are attractive to the unemployed (the outsiders) but which do not threaten the incomes of existing worker or capitalist partners (the insiders).

It is, therefore, a basic feature of Agathotopian policy to encourage such discriminatory arrangements as well as to encourage the acceptance of risks of variation in rates of remuneration. The measures already discussed in connection with the distribution of income and the alleviation of risk-bearing are also helpful to ease the acceptance of discrimination in rates of remuneration. Measures such as a widespread ownership of capital and thus of income from capital and the payment of a tax-free fixed Social Dividend all serve to reduce the importance of earned relative to other income. These measures can thus help to promote a desirable shift of emphasis away from institutional arrangements for setting high levels of remuneration for work on to fiscal and similar measures as the main instruments for the maintenance of standards of living and for the distribution of income. The more this happens the easier it is for work and the reward for work to be regarded with less rigid commitment. Part-time work becomes more frequent and differences in the remunerations offered to different workers joining an enterprise at different times and in different conditions can become more acceptable.

The Budgetary Implications

The Agathotopians have had to face the hideous expense involved in solving these two problems of the redistribution of income and wealth and of risk-bearing. All the measures mentioned above involve in one way or another fiscal measures of taxation or levies to promote redistribution in the ownership of wealth, to finance social services, or to redistribute income between individuals. It is all too easy to build up a rosy picture of these three forms of redistributive measures without due attention to the financial cost. It is not difficult to produce an attractive redistributive programme the finance of which would involve a 90 per cent rate of tax on the total income of the community. There is a very real trade-off between efficiency and equality in the community. If one paid every citizen a Social Dividend equal to the national average product of industry per head whether the citizen worked or not, one would need a tax of 100 per cent on all production to finance it. No citizen would have any incentive to earn any extra income by going out to work. The national product and thus the Social Dividend would fall to zero. There would be complete equality at zero income per head. There is a similar trade-off between efficiency and the alleviation of risk-bearing. The payment of a tax-free Social Dividend sounds a very attractive way of mitigating the burden of risk-bearing; but even if it is paid only at a moderate rate it is an alarmingly expensive form of remedy.

This raises two issues which the Agathotopians have had to face: first, the moral-political problem of deciding how much efficiency one should be prepared to sacrifice for how much equality and for how much promotion of partnership; and, second, the economic-political problem of the choice of means for a given promotion of equality and of partnership which will avoid or minimise any adverse effects upon efficiency. A major feature of the Agathotopian reaction to this second issue has been to seek a new source of revenue through the State enjoying the beneficial ownership (without incurring the day-to-day management) of a substantial proportion of the island's capital wealth.

The rest of this Part III is devoted to a more detailed description of the distinctive features of Agathotopian institutions and policies which have been designed to promote a true partnership economy with an acceptable balance between the conflicting considerations outlined above.

The Institutions of Agathotopia

(1) Discriminating Labour-Capital Partnerships and the Stabilisation of the Money GDP as a means of Maintaining Full Employment without Inflation

The competitive sector of the Agathotopian economy is marked by a widespread structure of Discriminating Labour-Capital Partnerships at the individual enterprise level. They do not cover the whole of Agathotopian economic activity. Many branches of the public service including, for example, defence, police, and administration of other services cannot be run by individual competitive private partnerships, even though a considerable range of relevant activities are contracted out by the public authorities to such private partnerships. Moreover there are activities which must be run on so great a monopolistic scale or which carry such external advantages or disadvantages to society that it is thought best to operate them as public nationalised monopolies.

There is no compulsion on private enterprise to take the form of Discriminating Labour-Capital Partnerships, and in fact there are many instances of familiar Capitalist Companies and Labour-Managed Cooperatives in the Agathotopian economy. But the Agathotopians have succeeded in transforming a very large part of the private sector of their economy into Discriminating Labour-Capital Partnerships by offering important tax advantages to such enterprises. These fiscal privileges are, however, strictly restricted to those partnerships whose constitution effectively introduces the principle of discrimination in their arrangements for the pay of working members.

In the absence of such discrimination Labour-Capital Partnerships could be very restrictive and lead to heavy unemployment and rapid cost inflation. The existing partners in any such enterprise, both workers and owners would have an incentive to restrict output, to limit the number of working partners, and to raise selling prices so long as they could thereby raise the dividend per share certificate. With all such enterprises acting in this way there would be grave danger of a cumulative inflation of prices combined with heavy unemployment throughout the economy. This outcome would be reversed if the principle of discrimination were effectively applied in an economy in which the total of money expenditures on the products of industry was also being effectively controlled. Suppose that in such conditions the existing worker partners had managed to inflate prices by restricting the size of the working partnership to that number which would serve to maximise labour pure profit per working partner. They would then find that they had an incentive to take on more working partners, to expand output and to reduce selling prices just so long as new working partners were willing to join the partnership for a rate of reward which was less than what the product of their work would add to the net revenue of the enterprise. The existing shareholders would thus all stand to gain so long as there were available any unemployed citizens who would welcome work at a rate of reward which was less than what their work would add to the net revenue of existing Labour-Capital Partnerships.

In combination with a widespread structure of Discriminating Partnerships the Agathotopians have accordingly adopted the stabilisation of their money GDP on a steady 5 per-cent-per-annum growth path as one of the major objectives of their monetary and fiscal policies. (Other objectives of their financial policies are discussed below.) Against this steady but restrained rise in the total money expenditure on the products of labour the expansionary forces of successful Discriminating Partnerships prevent the growth of any excessive unemployment without any undue inflationary developments.

(2) Savings-Exempt Income Tax combined with Taxes on the Transfer of Wealth as a means for Promoting the Widespread Ownership of Capital Wealth

In Agathotopia there is a much more equal spread in the ownership of private wealth than there is with us. Their problem was to devise means by which any such wide spread of ownership might be attained and indeed maintained when once it was attained. For there are very powerful influences in a free competitive society for the restoration of inequalities. By luck or special ability and enterprise some individuals may earn more than others by their work or invest their wealth more productively; others by bad luck or less than average ability may do worse. But those who happen to do well will be in a much better position to save more and thus to do still better, while those who do badly may actually have to live on what wealth they do possess. There are thus forces which make the wealthy more wealthy and the poor still poorer. If there is freedom of inheritance these differences are handed on; and those citizens who inherit much are in an easy position to accumulate still more wealth. Thus arrangements were sought not only to achieve a more equal distribution of the ownership of property but also to maintain the situation once it had been achieved.

They considered the merits of a system which exempted from tax all the savings of the poor and financed this tax exemption of the savings of the poor by a progressive tax on all personal holdings of wealth above a certain limit. For the poor the accumulation of wealth would be made easy; for the wealthy it would be more difficult to add yet more to their wealth. One way to do this would be to replace any existing income tax by a tax on expenditure on consumption. The procedure would be to assess as before each taxpayer's income, to add to that sum the proceeds of any sales of the taxpayer's property, and to subtract from that sum the cost of the acquisition of any new items of capital wealth. The result would be to levy tax on the net inflow of purchasing power which had been used to spend on consumption. All net saving would be exempt from tax.

If with such an arrangement which relieved all net savings from tax there were combined a tax on all holdings of wealth which exceeded a certain limit, it would be easier for everyone to accumulate wealth up to that limit and more difficult for everyone to accumulate wealth beyond that limit.

The Agathotopians did arrange for all net savings to be exempt from income tax, but they considered that there would be serious disadvantages in a heavy wealth tax. It would make it more difficult for a successful enterpriser, whether or not he or she was sharing that success with other partners, to find the funds to expand an existing adventurous business. In the environment of successful business enterprises which it was an important objective of the competitive market partnership economy to promote, such a stop to the accumulation of private wealth would have serious disadvantages.

For this reason it was thought preferable not to rely on an annual wealth tax on large holdings of wealth or at least to restrict such a levy to very moderate rates of tax. In its place they preferred to rely on duties levied on the passing of the ownership of large holdings of wealth from one owner to another on the occasion of death or of a gift *inter vivos*.

They combined this taxation of gifts and bequests with a low rate of tax levied annually on all personal holdings of wealth above a low exemption level. For the assessment of the annual wealth tax they accept each citizen's personal valuation of his or her various assets. But there is an added provision that the State can purchase any such asset at a price 10 per cent above its declared valuation, thus setting a strict limit to undervaluation. This low rate of annual wealth tax raises a significant revenue. (Thus a tax of 5 per mille on the capital value of an asset which produces a 5 per-cent-per-annum yield represents a tax of 10 per cent on that annual income.) But the tax has a most important secondary purpose in providing an inexpensive but reliable valuation of capital assets for the administration of the savings-exempt income tax and the taxation of gifts and bequests.[9]

The Agathotopians argued that such an arrangement would not interfere unduly with the accumulation of capital by an adventurous and successful entrepreneur over his or her lifetime; but the concentration of wealth through inheritance would be reduced, and the State would receive a revenue which would at least be sufficient to set against the loss of tax on the net savings of other citizens.

(3)   The Payment of a Tax-Free Social Dividend for the Promotion of Equality, the Alleviation of Risk-Bearing, the Improvement of Incentives for Low Earnings, and the Simplification of the Welfare State

In Agathotopia a tax-free Social Dividend is paid to every citizen according to the citizen's age and family status but without any other conditions. Two of the basic reasons for this institution have already been noted; namely, (i) the equalising effect of providing everyone with the same basic income; and

(ii) the reduction of risk when some part of income is unaffected by variations in a worker's remuneration for work.

Social Benefits which are conditional upon the recipient being unemployed or being in need because of inadequate alternative income imply serious disincentives for accepting low earnings. The Conditional Benefit may be one which like unemployment benefit will be entirely removed if the recipient finds work or may be one which will be reduced pound for pound as the recipient increases his or her income from additional outside earnings. A Social Dividend may be regarded as an Unconditional Social Benefit which is not removed or reduced because of increased earnings.

The payment of a substantial Social Dividend will diminish disincentives against acceptance of earned pay even if the Dividend is in itself inadequate and has to be supplemented by a Conditional Social Benefit. Thus, for example, a recipient of a Social Dividend of 80 supplemented by a Conditional Benefit of 20 will have an incentive to take outside earnings so long as those earnings after deduction of Income Tax are greater than 20; but if he or she had relied for the whole 100 on a Conditional Benefit, there would be no incentive to accept any outside earnings less than 100.

The Agathotopians have, however, in the end been able to pay Social Dividends on a sufficient scale to replace a very great range of the social benefits that would otherwise be needed to support the unemployed, the sick, the children and the old who were without adequate maintenance. The great obstacle to this happy institution of paying unconditional tax-free Social Dividends on what may be called an 'adequate' scale was, of course, the hideous expense involved and the consequent problem of raising the revenue needed for their payment. Indeed the payment of a fully adequate Social Dividend was ultimately achieved only at the cost of the most heroic and controversial fiscal measures. It is of interest, therefore, to note the Agathotopian history of the development of this institution of 'adequate' Social Dividends.[10]

The first stage in this development took the form of a gradual elimination of all Conditional Benefits (such as unemployment or sickness benefit or State payments in respect of old age and retirement pensions) which were conditional on anything other than the lack of adequate sources of other income. These Benefits were all replaced by a single Conditional Benefit, set at an 'adequate' level but withdrawn pound for pound as other income was available. This transformation was accompanied by a raising of personal allowances under the Income Tax regime to equality with the universal Conditional Benefit, with the result that a citizen received Conditional Benefit to make up for any deficiency of earnings or other income below the adequate standard level but paid Income Tax only on earnings or other income which was in excess of the adequate standard. This transformation of the tax-benefit system was expensive in so far as the adequate standard was set at a rather generous level and was payable to all so that no citizens were left without an adequate income; it was also particularly expensive in that it raised personal allowances under the Income Tax to the adequate standard level, thus reducing the tax burden on all the richer members who enjoyed the raising of their personal allowances; but it saved much expense in that the unemployed, sick, or old who had other adequate means received no cash support from the State. The transformation simplified very considerably the administrative problem in that it removed the whole apparatus of bureaucratic control needed to ensure that beneficiaries were genuinely unemployed or sick. It increased the responsibility of the Income Tax authorities who already needed in principle to assess all personal incomes but whose responsibility at the lower end of the income scale became so much the more important. The great problem which this first stage of development left totally unsolved was the complete disincentive for citizens at the lower end of the income scale to make any effort to earn or acquire additional income unless it took them beyond the adequate standard level and thus took them out of the poverty trap.

The second stage was to introduce Social Dividends at a moderate rate. These payments were financed from four sources: (i) the abolition of tax-free personal allowances under the existing income tax arrangements, so that all income (other than the Social Dividend) became subject to tax; (ii) the reduction of the existing Conditional Benefit by an amount equal to the Social Dividend; (iii) the levying of tax on the increase of incomes earned by those taking low paid jobs which they had not sought so long as their support had been conditional upon their not earning other income; and (iv) the moderate raising of rates of taxation (or rather the sacrifice of certain reductions of tax rates which would otherwise have been possible at that particular time). This moderate advance was found to have appreciable, albeit moderate, advantageous effects on the distribution of incomes, the alleviation of risk-bearing, and incentives to accept low paid or part time employment.

In the third stage, the Agathotopians set out gradually to raise rates of taxation until the revenue was sufficient to finance Social Dividends at a level which would be, in general, adequate to maintain citizens who had no other income. As they proceeded on this path they naturally experienced, as they had expected, a further equalisation of incomes. They also experienced a further alleviation of risk-bearing on a scale which they had not expected because they had overlooked the fact that risk-bearing is alleviated not only by the receipt of a larger constant assured element of income but also by the higher marginal rates of tax on all other incomes which are needed to raise the revenue to finance the higher rate of Social Dividend.

In fact the higher the rate of tax, the less does an earner gain by earning more (since a higher proportion of his or her extra earnings is paid to the State in tax) and the less does he or she lose by earning less (since a higher proportion of the loss is offset by a reduction of tax payment). The development of the Social Dividend regime was thus found to alleviate risk both by making a larger proportion of post tax income take the form of a tax-free constant income and also by reducing the effect of variations in the remaining element of income by linking variations in earnings with offsetting variations in tax liabilities.

Alas, however, the Agathotopians had to call a halt to this general development long before the Social Dividends had reached an adequate level, simply because the marginal rates of tax on increased earnings and profits combined with the assurance of the substantial unconditional income represented by the Social Dividend introduced an unacceptably large general disincentive for enterprising work and investment.

In the fourth stage the Agathotopians raised additional revenue by imposing a substantial tax surcharge on the first slice of every taxpayer's income. This meant that, after receipt of the tax-free Social Dividend, the taxpayer not merely lost tax exemption from the first slice of earnings or other income (which he or she had previously enjoyed in the form of personal tax allowances) but actually paid an exceptionally high rate of tax on this first slice of such income.

It may at first sight seem very anomalous that the Agathotopians should have instituted such a surcharge which involves levying a higher rate of tax on low incomes than on the higher incomes. But the justification of the system becomes apparent if one compares the three systems of (1) a pure Social Dividend System, (2) a pure Conditional Benefit System, and (3) a Social Dividend System with a Surcharge on the first slice of income from other sources.

(1) A pure Social Dividend System implies paying every citizen an adequate Social Dividend of, say, £100 and then taxing all other income (earnings, dividends, interest, rent etc) at, say 55 per cent for its finance.

(2) A pure Conditional Benefit System implies offering to every citizen an adequate Benefit of, say, £100 but then deducting from the citizen's benefit 100 per cent of any other income which that citizen may receive, until the point is reached when the Conditional Benefit payable to him or her is reduced to zero. The finance of such a scheme might require a rate of tax of only, say, 25 per cent on all other sources of income in order to finance such limited amounts of Conditional Benefit as remain payable to those citizens whose other sources of income were less than £100. Such an arrangement is the exact equivalent of a Social Dividend of £100 financed partly by a combined rate of tax of 100 per cent on the first slice of a citizen's other sources of income (i.e. by the 25 per cent rate of income tax plus a Surcharge of 75 per cent on the first £100 of earnings etc) and partly by a rate of tax of 25 per cent on all other sources of income in excess of the first £100 slice.

(3) A Social Dividend scheme with a more moderate Surcharge on the first £100 of earnings etc, will lie in between the extremes of (1) and (2). Thus for example there might be a Surcharge of 15 per cent (instead of 75 per cent) on the first £100 slice of income together with a general rate of income tax of 45 per cent on all income other than the Social Dividend. In this case the combined tax rate payable on the first £100 slice of income would be 60 per cent (i.e. 45 per cent + 15 per cent) and on income above £100 would be 45 per cent.

In all three cases all citizens are guaranteed a basic standard income of £100, financed in Scheme (1) by a tax of 55 per cent on all other sources of income, in Scheme (2) by a tax of 100 per cent on all other sources of income below £100 and a tax of 25 per cent on all other sources of income above £100, and (3) Scheme 3 by a tax of 60 per cent on all other sources of income below £100 combined with a tax of 45 per cent on all other sources of income above £100. If a tax rate of 55 per cent on the great majority of incomes above the £100 adequate subsistence level is found to have an unacceptable disincentive effect on work and enterprise, a move from Scheme 1 to Scheme 3 may enable the rate of tax on higher levels of income to be reduced from 55 per cent to a tolerable level of 45 per cent. This would still enable those at the bottom end of the scale to supplement their basic £100 with 40 per cent of any other sources of income, whereas a move to Scheme 2 would reduce their total incomes to the dead level of £100, thereby eliminating all incentives and reducing their standards of living to the basic minimum. If a pure Social Dividend is too expensive, a Social Dividend with a Surcharge on low incomes may be much better both for incentives and for the distribution of income than a pure Conditional Benefit system.

The outstanding revenue effect of the Surcharge on the first slice of income is that all citizens at the upper end of the income scale pay what amounts to a fixed 'poll tax' (i.e. the Surcharge on £100), which will enable a considerable revenue to be raised from such citizens without any rise of the marginal rate of tax on their other sources of income. In this way additional revenue can be raised from the rich without any disincentive effects—indeed perhaps with some slight improvement in incentives to earn more in order to make up for the 'poll tax' loss of income.

The Agathotopians found that such a Surcharge greatly relieved the situation. But, of course, the greater the relief of disincentives at the top end of the income scale brought about by raising the Surcharge with its 'poll tax' effects, the greater the disincentive effects and the lower the raising of standards at the lower end of the scale. It remains a matter of great controversy in the Agathotopian community whether the inevitable disincentive effects of high tax rates either at the upper or at the lower end of the income scale in fact justified the setting of the basic minimum at the generous level required to satisfy the requirements of a fully adequate standard of living.

In a fifth stage of development of their Social Dividend regime the Agathotopians found an entirely new and revolutionary source of revenue which much relieved the situation. This source of revenue took the form of the socialisation of the beneficial ownership (without incurring any of the management) of some 50 per cent of the national wealth of the community, a change of such basic structural importance as to merit discussion as a wholly novel institutional feature of the Agathotopian economy.

(4)   The Socialisation of the Beneficial Ownership (without the Management) of One Half of the Island's Capital Assets as a Source of Revenue for the Finance of the Social Dividend

The Agathotopian State itself owns some 50 per cent of the capital wealth of the community and uses the revenue from the return on this capital to help to finance the Social Dividend. At present in the typical capitalist economy the State far from being a net owner of capital assets in fact is often on balance a debtor to the private sector of the community. The private sector owns more capital assets than the total real assets of the community because it owns also the net National Debt issued by the governmental sector to the private sector. In Agathotopia there is no net National Debt; in its place there is a net National Asset equal to one half of the real assets of the community. The private sector owns only one half of the real assets of the community instead of an amount of wealth equal to the whole of the real assets of the community plus the net National Debt of the governmental sector. The absence of a net National Debt and the additional ownership by the State of wealth equivalent to one half of the real wealth of the community means, of course, that the government loses the revenue from any taxes which would otherwise have been levied on the interest on the National Debt and on dividends or rents received on the other transferred assets. But there is a net gain equal to the post-tax return on what would otherwise have been a National Debt and on one half of the real assets of the economy, a revenue which is used in Agathotopia to help to finance the Social Dividend.

In Agathotopia, however, the government plays no direct part in the management of the partnership enterprises or other private concerns the capital of which it owns indirectly. There is a free and very vigorous competitive capital market and Stock Exchange on which private individuals and institutions freely deal in respect to the 50 per cent of the real assets of the community which they own. The government invests its ownership of the other 50 per cent of the community's real assets in competitive unit trusts and similar competitive investment institutions which merge the government's funds with the private funds in the search of a high yield on the funds so employed. Thus indirectly the Agathotopian government receives the yield on the Capital Share Certificates of various Labour-Capital Partnerships and on the capital resources of other private concerns without taking any direct part in the management of the economy's competitive private enterprises. It is indeed an unwritten rule of the Agathotopian economy that the government should leave the competitive market alone but that it should be the beneficial owner of a large part of the community's wealth so that the income from such wealth can be equally distributed to all citizens in the form of a Social Dividend.

To many of us living at present in a capitalist mixed economy this must appear a topsy-turvy form of nationalisation or socialisation of property. In the UK, for example, immediately after World War Two the Labour Government carried out a widespread programme of nationalisation of private enterprises, Coal Mines, Steel, Transport, Electricity etc. But in all these cases adequate compensation was paid to the private owners. The net result was that the government took over the management of the concerns while the previous private owners continued to enjoy the yield on the property indirectly in the form of interest on the new National Debt issued in compensation. The Agathotopian form of socialisation is to take over the yield on the property, but to leave the management in private competitive hands.

The Agathotopians are, however, experiencing one difficulty in achieving this divorce between management and beneficial ownership of socialised assets. There is a wide range of capital assets in owner-occupied dwellings, owner-managed farms, small partnership enterprises etc, for the value of which there are no day-to-day quotations on the Stock Exchange or other similar capital market organisations. By investing its 50 per cent share of the total capital assets of the community exclusively in marketable assets the State threatens to swamp the Stock Exchange and similar organisations and to leave private owners of capital with only the range of less liquid non-marketable assets to hold. This threatens one of the basic objectives of the Agathotopian economy which is to have a flourishing and flexible private capital market of a kind which will make it possible for private enterprise easily to market its capital assets. The Agathotopians desire the Stock Exchange and similar markets for capital assets to have a very large private component.

For this reason they are considering the possibility of devising a form of tax which will enable them in effect to transfer part or the whole of the State's beneficial ownership of marketable Stock Exchange assets into beneficial part ownership of all capital assets whether marketable or non-marketable. To acquire an indirect participation of, say, 10 per cent in the beneficial ownership of all assets the procedure would be as follows. There would need to be a valuation of all real income-bearing assets. The State would pay a subsidy to the owner of each such asset of 10 per cent of its value. The funds needed for this subsidy would be obtained by the sale of part of the excessively large State holding of marketable assets. Thereafter all assets would be subject to a 10 per cent tax on their net income yield, there being an agreed formulation for the rate of yield to be assumed for tax purposes on owner-occupied dwellings and similar assets. This tax on the yield of all income-bearing real assets would be subject to 100 per cent initial tax allowances, in the sense that all owners of such assets could deduct from the gross yield earned on the assets not only the cost of maintaining and replacing the assets but also the cost of acquiring additional real assets of this kind. On the other hand, the taxable yield on such assets would also include any proceeds from the disposal of such assets. The implication of this system would be that the State acquired a 10 per cent participation in the ownership of all such assets, having 'purchased' this ownership by a subsidy to the owners on the first take-over and later by a remission of tax equal to 10 per cent of the cost of new additional assets. The State would then receive in revenue 10 per cent of the net yield on any such assets.[11]

(5) Budgetary Problems in Agathotopia and the Complexity of Agathotopian Fiscal Policy

In Agathotopia there are three exceptional features which, in comparison with the experience in a typical capitalist mixed economy, impose a heavy burden on the central government's budget. (i) There is a very heavy burden to carry in the form of the payment to all citizens of a Social Dividend on a scale adequate to support a decent standard of living. Even after allowance for the abolition of all other forms of social benefit this constitutes an extremely heavy addition to public expenditure in comparison with the normal expenditures on social benefits in a typical capitalist mixed economy. (ii) In addition the Agathotopian budget needs on average year after year to run a budget surplus on current account; in a growing economy it is necessary for the Agathotopian State to acquire new capital assets equal to one half of the nation's total savings, so as to maintain its beneficial ownership of one half of the country's growing national wealth. (iii) Moreover, it needs to raise revenue from some other source to make up for the fact that the Agathotopian income tax regime exempts all savings from tax in order to make easier the accumulation of capital wealth by the poorer members of society.

In order to keep marginal tax rates as low as possible the Agathotopians do all they can to prevent erosion of the tax base. Thus they impute a realistic taxable rent to the enjoyment of the owner-occupied dwellings and owner-managed farm lands; and, in their savings-exempt income tax, any capital gains which are realised for expenditure on consumption are automatically included in the tax base. They enjoy considerable administrative savings through the abolition of social benefits of a kind which depend upon the policing of specific conditions such as involuntary unemployment or genuine sickness; but they have used much of these resources to monitor the black economy, tax evasion of every kind being much better policed and much more heavily penalised than in the UK. In their general economic policies they concentrate on taxing that which is socially undesirable rather than subsidising that which is socially desirable, traffic congestion being tackled by exceptionally heavy taxation of the congesting use of private cars rather than by the subsidisation of public transport. They protect the countryside by taxing its obnoxious treatment rather than by subsidising farmers to produce unwanted supplies. They obtain a substantial revenue from a tax on expensive advertisement which they regard as a social nuisance and a waste of resources; in their opinion, it represents a mutually destructive and therefore ineffective means by which producers attempt to poach customers from each other in a way which, unlike a reduction of selling prices, confers no real benefit upon the consumers; it merely persuades them to vie with each other in the purchase of things which they would not otherwise want and which in many cases they cannot really afford. On business concerns they levy what corresponds to a Corporation Tax, from which Discriminating Labour-Capital Partnerships are exempt.

In addition to these general principles the Agathotopians have introduced three special measures in an attempt to alleviate the exceptionally heavy charges which it has to meet. (i) They raise a substantial revenue from the taxation of capital wealth. This takes two forms, (a) they levy a low annual tax on all personal holdings of wealth above a low exempt level and (b) they impose an important tax on all transfers of wealth by gift or bequest above a low exempt level. (ii) By maintaining a socialisation of the beneficial ownership of a net National Asset equal to one half of the nation's total wealth they avoid budgetary expenditure equal to the post tax payments of interest on what in a typical capitalist mixed economy might have been the net National Debt, and gain the post tax yield on its net National Asset. (iii) They raise a substantial Surcharge on the first slice of all personal incomes other than the tax-free Social Dividend.

However, in spite of these three substantial alleviations the Agathotopians have been able to maintain the adequate Social Dividend regime only at the expense of a fairly high general rate of savings-exempt income tax.

In addition to these exceptional fiscal burdens on the Agathotopian budget the fiscal regime in Agathotopia has to face a rather more complex task than is the case elsewhere. In the capitalist mixed economy it is natural to think of the three instruments of Wage and Price Setting Institutions, Monetary Policy, and Fiscal Policy as means of influencing the three macroeconomic targets of Maintenace of a High and Stable Level of Employment, Control of Inflation, and Influence on Economic Growth through the Accumulation of Capital. Fiscal Policy is broadly interpreted in this connection as the determination of the Budget Balance (i.e. the pouring or sucking of purchasing into or out of the private sector of the economy).

This is, of course, not the sole interest in Fiscal Policy in the capitalist mixed economy. In particular the actual forms and levels of government expenditure and of tax revenues within any given Budget Balance are considered in their effects on at least two further macroeconomic issues, namely the general effects on the Distribution of Incomes and on the Incentives to Work, Enterprise and Investment.

In the Agathotopian economy all these same financial instruments and objectives are operative. But Fiscal Policy is still further complicated by an Agathotopian interest not only in the growth of the total capital assets of the economy but also in the distribution of the beneficial ownership of such assets as between the private and public sectors. In essence while the capitalist economy is concerned with a single Wealth Target (e.g. the community's total capital assets) the Agathotopian economy is concerned with two Wealth Targets, the total accumulation of assets and the distribution of the ownership of such assets as between the private and public sectors.

To meet this twofold wealth objective the Agathotopians try to distinguish between those taxes which are likely to be paid largely at the expense of the taxpayer's real consumption (such as the savings-exempt income tax) and those which are likely to be paid largely at the expense of the taxpayer's savings or holdings of wealth (such as the tax on transfers of wealth). By controlling the size of its budget surplus the Agathotopian government aims to control the growth of its own holding of wealth; by choosing a suitable mix of consumption and capital taxes in the composition of the necessary revenue it aims at achieving simultaneously the desired level of private savings. They do not expect perfection. The level of any social dividend; the level of any special levy on the first slice of income or expenditure; the level of government expenditures on defence, health, education, and other services; the structure, rates and progression of rates of tax on savings-exempt income, on wealth and on transfers of wealth; all these they realise will have effects on distribution, on incentives and on the provision of both public and private savings. They are continuously revising a structured package of these various items in order to provide not a perfect distribution of income and wealth, nor a complete absence of economic disincentives, nor the ideal level of total savings, nor its ideal distribution between public and private savings but rather to find the least undesirable package of imperfect distribution, imperfect incentives, imperfect level and imperfect distribution of saving between public and private savings. Agathotopia is a Good Place to live in, but it is, alas, not Utopia.

Part IV The Transition to the Partnership Economy

In the island of Agathotopia the acquisition by the State of one half of the economy's wealth is already past history. It occurred more than a century ago and the trauma of the event has been totally forgotten. The institution is just taken for granted. If, however, we in our capitalist mixed economies wished to reach an Agathotopian type of economy, how could we make the transition? In particular how could we make the transfer of the beneficial ownership of the National Debt plus one half of the real wealth of the community from the private to the public sector of the economy?

One possibility might be a once-for-all cataclysmic Capital Levy by which a given amount of wealth, on a progressive scale according to the size of the individual private holdings of property, was transferred from private to public ownership. This would involve a gigantic social revolution. History suggests that the immediate uncompromising forcing of major changes on this scale against fiercely held opposition inevitably leads to unforeseen disastrous results. Situations of traumatic change may arise for other reasons. At the end of World War Two it was reasonable to consider the possibility of a large-scale Capital Levy to rid the country of a large part of the National Debt incurred during the War. But a vast once-for-all transfer in normal times could have disastrous effects upon the stability of society.

This means that the transition to Agathotopian arrangements is going to take a long time. Some form of continuing budget surplus will be needed in order gradually to redeem National Debt and to acquire instead a net National Asset. In so far as private savings are considered to be insufficient to meet the national wealth target, it is appropriate that the budget surplus should be raised by taxes which restrain private consumption. In so far as private savings are considered to be adequate, shift of wealth from the private to the public sector can be achieved by financing the budget surplus from taxes which are likely to be paid out of private savings or holdings of wealth. In either case the interest on National Debt will gradually fall and/or the return on National Assets will gradually rise. The ever greater budgetary ease can then be used partly to improve a Social Dividend payment and partly to raise the annual budget surplus and thus to speed up the process of transfer of property. There is great virtue in compound interest. It can set in motion a reliable gradual improvement in social welfare. The first steps on the journey should be the hardest.

The approaches to the other Agathotopian institutions can all be taken gradually. Labour-Capital Partnerships can be developed gradually at the enterprise level. Reforms of taxation of income and of transfers of wealth can be introduced by stages so as to encourage a wider spread of the ownership of property. A Social Dividend can be started on a very moderate scale financed out of the abolition of existing personal allowances under the income tax, by the reduction of other social benefits, and by some moderate increases of tax rates supplemented at some stage with an element of special levy on the first slice of other income. If the journey is taken at a gentle pace, one can hope ultimately to reach Agathotopian conditions without too much strain on the way.

Appendix A Factors Restricting the Replacement of Retiring Worker Partners

In the main text it was argued that the adoption of the rule of redistribution for the treatment of the pure-profit of retiring worker partners and, to a lesser extent, the adoption of the rule of cancellation for this purpose might impede the expansionary forces in a Discriminating Labour-Capital Partnership. The younger recently engaged partners might oppose the engagement of new partners in order to restrict the number of future potential recipients of any pure profit which was released by older worker partners on their retirement.

The purpose of this Appendix is to analyse this potential motive for restriction in the case of the rules of redistribution and of cancellation. We illustrate these forces by examining a particular example of the occurrence of pure profit in a Discriminating Labour-Capital Partnership.

In Table 1 we consider a partnership in which there are m teams of working partners of equal sizes. Team m was engaged at the beginning of this year (Year 1), team $m-1$ was engaged last year, team $m-2$, was engaged two years ago; and so on. Team 1 will retire at the end of this year. For many years up to and including Year–1 this partnership has covered its costs but has made no pure profit so that each team of workers has been receiving a zero pure profit as indicated in the column headed Year–1. In Year 0 there is a sudden but lasting improvement in the performance of the partnership; a large pure profit is made; each working partner's share of this pure profit amounts to B' as shown in the column headed Year 0.

At the beginning of Year 1 the old Team 1 retires, each of the other teams moves one step up the team index, leaving team m to be replaced by a new team which on the discriminatory principle does not share in the existing pure profit. Each of the other $m-1$ teams receives in addition to its existing pure profit of B' a supplement equal to $(1-\sigma)/(m-1)$ of the B' which is surrendered by the retiring team 1 of Year 0. In this expression σ measures the proportion of the benefit which seeps to holders of Capital Share Certificates. Thus σ will be zero if (as with the rule of redistribution) all the retiring team's pure profit is distributed in equal amounts among the remaining worker partners and will be equal to $\bar{\sigma}$, the ratio of Capital Share Certificates to total Share Certificates, if (as with the rule of cancellation) the

46

retiring team has simply to surrender for cancellation all its holding of Labour Share Certificates. With $B = B' \mu_1$ and $\mu_1 = (m - \sigma)/(m - 1)$, the distribution of pure profit among the worker partners will in Year 1 be as shown in the column headed Year 1.

The purpose of Table 1 is to consider the future prospects of those teams of 'old hands' who were already engaged in this partnership in Year 0. We are accordingly concerned only with the fortunes of those teams which lie above the heavy line sloping up Table 1 diagonally from left to right.

At the beginnning of Year 2 team 1 of Year 1 will retire releasing a pure profit of B to be distributed among the other $m - 1$ teams of Year 1. One of the beneficiaries of this redistribution will be the team of 'new hands' engaged at the beginning of Year 1 and lying below the heavy diagonal line in Table 1. Teams 2 to $m - 1$ of Year 1 will have become teams 1 to $m - 2$ of Year 2, each with $B + B(1 - \sigma)/(m - 1) = B\mu_1$.[12]

By a similar process the amount of pure profit for the remaining teams of 'old hands' will develop as shown in Table 1 for future years up to Year $m - 1$.

In Table 2 we start off with the same story as in Table 1 for all years up to and including Year 0; but we suppose now that at the beginning of Year 1 a decision had been taken to reduce the size of the partnership by one team by not replacing the retiring team 1 of Year 0. Thus in Table 2 after Year 0 production will be carried on by only $m - 1$ teams instead of m teams. If the marginal revenue product of the missing team had been more than its cost, its absence would mean some reduction in the partnership's pure profit. If we suppose that the absence of a single team caused a loss of total pure profit to the partnership of $\tilde{B}$, then $\tilde{B}(1 - \bar{\sigma})$ of this would be loss of pure profit to the working partners, so that there would be a loss of pure profit to each team of workers of $\delta = \tilde{B}(1 - \bar{\sigma})/(m - 1)$. In Table 2 accordingly for Year 1 we record each team of 'old hands' as enjoying a pure profit of $B - \delta$ instead of B as in Table 1.

Clearly the 'old hands' will suffer an immediate loss of pure profit if absence of the new team (which on the discriminating principle would have been paid only its cost) causes some reduction in the total pure profit available for distribution. But in future years this loss will to a smaller or greater extent be balanced for the 'old hands' by a gain from the fact that the pure profit enjoyed by a retiring member will be divided among only $m - 2$ instead of $m - 1$ teams. This development is shown in Table 2 which differs from Table 1 in only two respects: first, that each team of 'old hands' starts in Year 1 with a pure profit of $B - \delta$ instead of B; and, second, that a retiring working member's pure profit is distributed among $m - 2$ instead of $m - 1$ other teams so that $\mu_1 = 1 + (1 - \sigma)(m - 1) = (m - \sigma)/(m - 1)$ is replaced by $\mu_2 = 1 + (1 - \sigma)/(m - 2) = (m - 1 - \sigma)/(m - 2)$.

We can now use Tables 1 and 2 to compare the difference of the future prospects of any given team of 'old hands' at Year 1 as between the case of Table 1 in which it is decided to replace the retiring team and the case of Table 2 in which it is decided to reduce the future size of the partnership by one team.

TABLE 1 REDISTRIBUTION OF LABOUR PURE PROFIT WITH REPLACEMENT OF RETIRING TEAM

$$B = B'\mu_1 \qquad \mu_1 = 1 + \frac{1-\sigma}{m-1} = \frac{m-\sigma}{m-1}$$

Year \ Team	−1	0	1	2	3	4	...	m−2	m−1
1	0	B'	B	$B\mu_1$	$B\mu_1^2$	$B\mu_1^3$	...	$B\mu_1^{m-3}$	$B\mu_1^{m-2}$
2	0	B'	B	$B\mu_1$	$B\mu_1^2$	$B\mu_1^3$	...	$B\mu_1^{m-3}$	
3	0	B'	B	$B\mu_1$	$B\mu_1^2$	$B\mu_1^3$			
...	...	...	...	...	...	...			
m−3	0	B'	B	$B\mu_1$	$B\mu_1^2$				
m−2	0	B'	B	$B\mu_1$					
m−1	0	B'	B						
m	0	B'							

TABLE 2 REDISTRIBUTION OF LABOUR PURE PROFIT WITHOUT REPLACEMENT OF RETIRING TEAM

$$B = B^1_{\mu_1} \qquad \mu_1 = 1 + \frac{1-\sigma}{m-1} = \frac{m-\sigma}{m-1} \qquad \mu_2 = 1 + \frac{1-\sigma}{m-2} = \frac{m-1-\sigma}{m-2} \qquad \delta = \frac{\tilde{B}(1-\bar{\sigma})}{m-1}$$

Year / Team	−1	0	1	2	3	4	…	m−2	m−1
1	0	B'	$B-\delta$	$(B-\delta)\mu_2$	$(B-\delta)\mu_2^2$	$(B-\delta)\mu_2^3$	…	$(B-\delta)\mu_2^{m-3}$	$(B-\delta)\mu_2^{m-2}$
2	0	B'	$B-\delta$	$(B-\delta)\mu_2$	$(B-\delta)\mu_2^2$	$(B-\delta)\mu_2^3$	…	$(B-\delta)\mu_2^{m-3}$	
3	0	B'	$B-\delta$	$(B-\delta)\mu_2$	$(B-\delta)\mu_2^2$	$(B-\delta)\mu_2^3$			
…	…	…	…	…	…	…			
m−3	0	B'	$B-\delta$	$(B-\delta)\mu_2$	$(B-\delta)\mu_2^2$				
m−2	0	B'	$B-\delta$	$(B-\delta)\mu_2$					
m−1	0	B'	$B-\delta$						
m	0	B'							

Let $\rho = 1/(1+r)$ where r is the rate of interest at which working partners discount the future. In this case the Present Value of its pure profit for team $m-1$ in Table 1, to be expected at the beginning of Year 1 as the team moves up the heavy diagonal line is

$$B\{1 + \rho\mu_1 + (\rho\mu_1)^2 + \cdots + (\rho\mu_1)^{m-2}\} = B\frac{(\rho\mu_1)^{m-1} - 1}{\rho\mu_1 - 1} \qquad (1)$$

The corresponding value for the $m-1$ team of Year 1 on table 2 is

$$(B-\delta)\frac{(\rho\mu_2)^{m-1} - 1}{\rho\mu_2 - 1}.$$

Similar expressions can be found to express the present expected value of future pure profit for the pth team of Year 1 on Tables 1 and 2 by substituting in equation (1) the number of years' service still expected in the partnership (namely, p) for the number of years service expected by the $m-1$ team (namely, $m-1$).

Thus we can generalise by saying that the contraction of the partnership's worker membership by the failure to replace team 1 at the end of Year 0 should improve the future prospects for team p at the beginning of Year 1 if

$$(B-\delta)\frac{(\rho\mu_2)^p - 1}{\rho\mu_2 - 1} > B\frac{(\rho\mu_1)^p - 1}{\rho\mu_1 - 1}$$

i.e. if

$$\frac{\delta}{B} < \left\{1 - \frac{(\rho\mu_1)^p - 1}{\rho\mu_1 - 1} \middle/ \frac{(\rho\mu_2)^p - 1}{\rho\mu_2 - 1}\right\}. \qquad (2)$$

The outcome clearly depends upon whether or not the relative sacrifice of total worker's pure profit due to the reduction in the number of teams (δ/B) is outweighed by the advantage of having the pure profit of retiring members in future years distributed over a smaller number of beneficiaries ($\rho\mu_2 > \rho\mu_1$).

We have already noted that $\delta = \tilde{B}(1-\bar\sigma)/(m-1)$ so that we can write

$$\frac{\delta}{B} = \frac{\tilde{B}(1-\bar\sigma)}{(m-1)B} \qquad (3)$$

where $\tilde{B}$ is the excess of the Marginal Revenue Product over the cost (W) of one team, $\bar\sigma$ is the ratio of Capital Share Certificate to total Share Certificates, and $m-1$ measures the number of teams over which the loss of pure profit to the workers must be spread.

But $B = \mu_1 B' = (m-\sigma)/(m-1)B'$ as depicted in Table 1. If we write $B' = \beta W$ where W measures the cost element in the payment to a worker team so that β measures the ratio of the initial pure profit per team of workers (B') to the team's cost (W) we can rewrite (equation 3) as

$$\frac{\delta}{B} = \frac{\tilde{B}}{W} \cdot \frac{(1-\bar\sigma)}{(m-\sigma)\beta} \qquad (4)$$

so that the condition for the team p to gain by the contraction of the membership is expressed by the inequality (2) can be rewritten as:

$$\frac{\tilde{B}}{W} < \frac{(m-\sigma)\beta}{1-\bar{\sigma}}\left\{1 - \frac{(\rho\mu_1)^p - 1}{\rho\mu_1 - 1}\bigg/\frac{(\rho\mu_2)^p - 1}{\rho\mu_2 - 1}\right\} \tag{5}$$

The term $\tilde{B}/W$ on the left hand side of (5) measures the relative excess of a team's marginal revenue product over a team's cost and this, if the number of teams is large, can be regarded as an approximate indication of the proportionate excess of a worker's marginal revenue product over a worker's cost. If worker partners had been taken on until the worker's marginal revenue product had been reduced to the level of the worker's cost, $\tilde{B}/W$ would be zero and it would clearly be in the interests of existing worker partners to restrict the size of the workers' membership. But as the number of worker partners was reduced the marginal revenue product of a worker would be raised, and it would be in the interest of the pth team of workers to vote for such contraction until $\tilde{B}/W$ were raised at least to the critical level indicated in (5).[13]

The critical condition in (5) depends basically upon the discriminatory principle that any new team is engaged in the first place at a remuneration which is equal to its cost, although the other pre-existing teams may in addition be enjoying various levels of pure profit. It is of interest to contrast the critical value of $\tilde{B}/W$ in (5) with the critical value of $\tilde{B}/W$ which would need to be reached to make it unattractive for existing worker partners to restrict the membership in a Non-Discriminating partnership; in such a partnership all worker partners, new and old, would receive 'equal pay for equal work' which implies that any available pure profit would be shared equally among them.

In such a Non-Discriminating partnership the pure profit per team would be increased by the non-replacement of a team so long as the loss of worker pure profit caused by the reduction of one team $\tilde{B}(1-\bar{\sigma})$ were less than the existing pure profit per team B'. With $B' = \beta W$ this means that in a Non-Discriminating partnership the condition (5) for the pth team to gain from a restriction of the number of teams would be replaced by the condition

$$\frac{\tilde{B}}{W} < \frac{\beta}{1-\bar{\sigma}} \tag{6}$$

which would also be relevant for the prospective fortunes not only of the pth team but of any one of the existing teams.

In Table 3 we give some numerical examples of the implications of the conditions expressed in the inequalities (5) and (6). We assume that the working life of a working partner in any given partnerships is 20 years so that $m = 20$ and that the partnership is 20 per cent capital intensive in the sense that the ratio of Capital Share Certificates to Total Share Certificates is 0.2. Thus $\mu_1 = (m-\sigma)/(m-1) = 19.8/19 = 1.042$ and $\mu_2 = (m-1-\sigma)/(m-2) = 18.8/18 = 1.044$ in the case in which all Labour Share Certificates of retiring members are surrendered and cancelled; and $\mu_1 = 20/19 = 1.053$

TABLE 3 CRITICAL VALUES OF $\tilde{B}/W$ BELOW WHICH RESTRICTION OF NUMBER
OF WORKER PARTNERS WOULD BE ATTRACTIVE

		$\sigma = 0$	$\sigma = 0.2$
Discriminating Partnership	$p = m-1 = 19$	0.125	0.098
	$p = m/2 = 10$	0.0625	0.049
Non-Discriminating Partnership		0.25	0.25

With $m = 20$, $\rho = 1/1.05$, and $\beta = 0.2$.

and $\mu_2 = 19/18 = 1.056$ in the case in which the pure-profit Labour Share Certificates of retiring members are not cancelled but are distributed among the remaining worker partners. We assume further that the rate of discount of future benefits by worker partners is 5 per cent per annum so that $\rho = 1/1.05$ and that in the initial situation of Year 0 the amount of pure profit per worker was 20 per cent of the cost element in the working partners income so that $\beta = 0.2$.

The following features may be noted:

(1) All the critical values of $\tilde{B}/W$ are > 0. That is to say that if there is no excess of Marginal Revenue Product over Cost for the marginal team it will in all cases be attractive to worker partners to reduce the size of the membership. Since there is no immediate loss of total pure profit, it will always be of interest to existing worker partners to have to share the profit of retiring members over a smaller number of remaining beneficiaries.

(2) There will therefore be a critical positive value for $\tilde{B}/W$ which is necessary to remove the motive for restriction of numbers. This critical value is in every case higher in a Non-Discriminating Partnership than in a corresponding Discriminating Partnership. Thus we may conclude that the adoption of the principle of discrimination will lead to an expansion of the number of working partners, but that in those cases in which the pure profit of retiring members reverts in whole or in part to the remaining partners, there will remain obstacles to the complete expansion up to the point at which the marginal revenue product of an additional partner is reduced to the cost of a new partner.

(3) However, the critical value of $\tilde{B}/W$ which will make restriction of numbers attractive in a Discriminating Partnership, is lower for existing partners who have few more years of service than for existing partners who have many more years of service (i.e. in the Table for workers with 10 years of service ahead it is roughly only half as high as for those with 19 years ahead). The older working partners have a smaller prospect of gaining from the retirements of still older partners than is the case with the younger

partners. Indeed, as can be seen clearly from Table 2 the partners who are on the point of retirement will have no incentive to oppose the employment of a new team unless that team's marginal revenue product was actually lower than its cost (i.e. unless $\tilde{B}$ and so δ were negative). If $\tilde{B}$ is positive those on the point of retirement would certainly lose if the team is not engaged, because they will have nothing to gain from the redistribution of any pure profit enjoyed by their younger colleagues.

(4) This fact that the attractiveness of restriction of entry of new partners will be greater to younger than to older partners means that there may be an important difference of interest within the working membership. Thus in Table 3 the majority of members (teams up to the tenth team) would vote for expansion so long as $\tilde{B}/W$ was greater than around 6 per cent, whereas the youngest members of the team would vote for expansion only if $\tilde{B}/W$ were over $12\frac{1}{2}$ per cent.

(5) The existence of seepage of the pure profit of retiring worker members to the benefit of capitalist members ($\sigma > 0$) will reduce the advantage to the worker members to restrict numbers, since they have less to gain from the pure profit of retiring members. In Table 3 the rise of seepage from 0 to 20 per cent will substantially reduce the critical level to which $\tilde{B}/W$ may fall without leading to a desire to restrict the engagement of new working partners. Even more important is the fact that as the years pass the incentive for restriction will diminish until it completely disappears as the seepage of pure profit to the capitalist members progressively reduces the amount of labour pure profit available for the future benefit of younger members. This important feature is not shown in Tables 1, 2, or 3 which refer only to the position of the pth team immediately after the first appearance of the labour pure profit.

(6) Inequalities (5) and (6) show clearly the fundamental importance of the factor β in determining the level of the critical value of $\tilde{B}/W$ in all cases. A doubling of β (the proportion of initial pure profit to cost) will in all cases double the level of the critical value of $\tilde{B}/W$. The greater the amount of pure profit available for future redistribution, the greater will be the attraction to restrict membership.

(7) Table 3 does not itself show the effect on the critical level of $\tilde{B}/W$ of a change in the discount rate r and so of the factor ρ. But from Tables 1 and 2 it can be clearly seen that if the future was discounted at an infinite rate all members of the partnership would be opposed to restriction unless δ were zero or negative. If δ (and so $\tilde{B}/W$) were positive every member would suffer the immediate loss due to the reduced total of pure profit resulting from the loss of one team's marginal contribution to the total pure profit. In fact the higher the rate of discount, the smaller will be the attraction of any future increase in pure profit per member arising from the future distribution of retiring members' pure profit among a smaller number of beneficiaries.

It is clear from the above analysis that the incentive to expand employment can vary very greatly according to the particular conditions of the particular partnership. For example in a case in which there was much workers' pure profit to distribute (a high β), no seepage to capitalists ($\sigma = 0$), and a low rate of time discount by working partners (a high ρ), the critical value of $\tilde{B}/W$ could be very high.

There is, however, one aspect of the problem which has so far been neglected and which in fact suggests that the degree of restriction on the size of a partnership's working membership will be less than has been suggested by the preceding analysis in this Appendix. We have treated W in this Appendix as a measure of the remuneration which must be paid during his first year of service to a newly engaged working partner. But if this partner has a prospect of receiving a considerable pure profit bonus in future years (i.e. if the present value of the engagement is exceptionally high) he may well be prepared to enter the partnership at an exceptionally low initial reward, i.e. an exceptionally low value of W and high value of $\tilde{B}$. But this will raise the actual level of $\tilde{B}/W$; it will mean that the loss of pure profit to the existing partners if they do not engage the new partner will be exceptionally high.

However, if the capital market is very imperfect and the newly-engaged working partner cannot borrow on good terms to make up for an exceptionally low starting remuneration, he may not be willing to accept an exceptionally low value of W. But this is only another way of saying that the working partners' rate of time discount is exceptionally high; and this in turn (instead of raising the actual level of $\tilde{B}/W$ through setting an exceptionally low level for W), will lower the critical value below which the existing $\tilde{B}/W$ must lie if there is to be a given attraction to restrict the working membership. Either way the restrictive influence is diminished.

In all cases it would appear that a Discriminating Labour-Capital Partnership would be less restrictive than a Non-Discriminating Partnership. But on the face of it, it would appear that a Capital Company would be even less restrictive than any Discriminating Partnership which operated on the rules of redistribution or of cancellation. At any given single level of W this would be true, since the owner of a Capitalist Company unlike the working partners of the Discriminating Partnership would have an incentive to expand employment so long as $\tilde{B}/W > 0$. This analysis rests, however, on the assumption that both the Capitalist Company and the Discriminating Partnership are confronted with the same value for W. In fact, as has been argued in the main text, the existing working partners (the insiders) in a Discriminating Labour-Capital Partnership will welcome outsiders who demand a low level of remuneration, whereas the insiders in a Capitalist Company will demand that outsiders be employed only at a high level of pay.

Appendix B The Characteristics of Various Social Dividend Schemes

This appendix is devoted to a description of the structure of different types of Social Dividend scheme. In order to compare the merits and demerits of the various schemes, it is useful to assume that each scheme is self-financing in the following sense. Each scheme will involve additional budgetary expenditure for the payment of the Social Dividend. It is assumed throughout this appendix that the additional revenue needed to balance the budget is raised by increasing the rates of Income Tax, all other tax rates and governmental expenditures remaining unchanged. All adult men and women are assumed to be assessed separately both for Income Tax and for receipt of social benefit, whatever their family circumstances; and children are all assumed to count as, say, one half an adult for receipt of social benefits.

A taxpayer's receipt of income from earnings and return on capital wealth before tax and social benefit will be called his or her Unadjusted Income, and after deduction of tax and payment of social benefit will be called his or her Adjusted Income. We examine in this appendix three kinds of adjustments to income which are specially designed to maintain the standards of living of those with little or no other income.

(1) Personal Tax Allowance

With a normal income tax regime we assume that a first slice of Unadjusted Income which we call the Personal Tax Allowance is exempt from income tax and that the same standard rate of tax is applied to every taxpayer's Unadjusted Income less Personal Tax Allowance.

(2) Conditional Benefits

Cash benefits may be paid to citizens in certain specific conditions, e.g. if the citizen is unemployed or sick. Or a cash benefit may be paid on condition that the recipient's receipt of any Unadjusted Income is deducted from the benefit. Both these types of social benefit we will call Conditional Benefits; but we will confine our analysis to the second type. Thus we may suppose that £100 is paid to a citizen who has no Unadjusted Income, but that this benefit is reduced pound for pound as his Adjusted Income rises from £0 to £100 at which point it is discontinued.

(3)   Unconditional Benefit or Social Dividend

If however a cash benefit is paid at a fixed rate to every taxpayer regardless of the level of his or her Unadjusted Income or of any other circumstances, we will call this a Social Dividend.

In general throughout this appendix we will assume that any Personal Tax Allowance, Conditional Benefit, or Social Dividend are all set at the same rate which is regarded as what is needed to enable a single adult citizen to maintain an adequate standard of living. We shall use this as the unit of measurement of income. Thus a citizen with an Unadjusted Income of 3 is a citizen whose pre-tax earnings and income from capital wealth are three times the minimum level assumed necessary to maintain an adequate living standard.

In Diagram 1 the line OBC would depict the situation under an Income Tax regime with a Personal Tax Allowance equal to 1 unit and a rate of tax of 25 per cent on all Unadjusted Income in excess of this 1 unit. With Unadjusted Income on the horizontal axis and Adjusted Income on the vertical axis, the line OBV would represent the level of Adjusted Income in the absence of any tax. With a Personal Allowance of 1 unit and a subsequent tax rate of 25 per cent the Adjusted Income moves up the line OB at a slope of 1 in 1 and from B moves up the line BC with a slope of 3 in 4. If the Personal Tax Allowance of 1 unit were replaced by a Conditional Benefit of 1 unit the Adjusted Income line would become the heavily marked line ABC. For all persons without any Unadjusted Income at the origin O a Conditional Benefit of OA would be paid and this would be reduced pound for pound as the citizen's Unadjusted Income moved up the line OB. At the point B the Conditional Social Benefit would have been reduced to zero and from B onwards the levy of tax would reduce the slope of BC to 3 in 4. In what follows we shall be comparing other regimes with this Conditional Benefit Regime and shall accordingly repeat the line ABC on all the following diagrams.

All citizens to the right of point M with Unadjusted Incomes above 1 unit will be paying tax, the revenue from which will lie in the horizontal hatched area {≡} between the lines BV and BC. All citizens to the left of point M will be receiving some Conditional Benefit, the expenditure on which will lie in the vertically hatched area { ||| } between the lines AB and OB. We are simply assuming that given this Conditional Benefit and the other elements of government expenditure (defence, health, education, etc) and given the other sources of government revenue (VAT, etc) an income tax rate of 25 per cent is sufficient to balance the budget. This simple assumption is chosen solely for illustrative purposes.

Indeed the choice of this low rate of 25 per cent should not be allowed to give the impression that to pay a universal Conditional Benefit at an adequate rate and to raise the Personal Tax Allowance up to this same adequate rate is anything but a very expensive policy. At the origin O are concentrated all those children, pensioners, sick, or unemployed who have no other sources of income; and this will include the unemployed who might be able to earn something less than 1 unit of income but who have no incentive to take such work as their pay would simply be deducted from the Conditional Benefit. Between O and M are all such citizens who have a small return from other sources. The bill for paying a Conditional Benefit at what is considered a fully adequate rate can be a very heavy one.

Moreover there is an additional cost if this involves raising the Personal Tax Allowance up to the same adequate level of 1 unit. Suppose, for example, that the Personal Tax Allowance had previously been set and were maintained at OA′, i.e. at half the fully adequate Conditional Benefit. The citizens' post tax income would then move up the line OB′C′. Up to the point X this inadequate income would be supported by the Conditional Benefit along the line AB. If now the Conditional Benefit were cut off at the point B, a citizen's Adjusted Income would fall abruptly from B to X as his or her Unadjusted Income rose from below to above the level OM. This would represent an unacceptable 'marginal tax rate' of more than 100 per cent; by earning more the citizen would reduce his or her spendable Adjusted Income. To prevent this anomalous situation the range of Unadjusted Income over which Conditional Benefit would be payable would have to be extended from AB to AY, so that Adjusted Income moved over the line AYC′.

Within the triangle B′BY the State would neither gain nor lose net revenue. If Income Tax were payable at source citizen's would be taxed in this area, but at the same time the payment of Conditional Benefit would have to be increased to offset the increased payment of tax. This would constitute a tiresome administrative arrangement with the authority in charge of Conditional Benefits paying out money for the recipients to pay over to the tax authority. But at the expense of this crude transfer of tax into benefit in this limited region, the maintenance of the Personal Tax Allowance at only half the level of the Conditional Benefit would raise a very substantial additional revenue for the State without any rise in the rate of tax above the existing rate of 25 per cent. The revenue whose loss would be avoided by not raising the Personal Tax Allowance up to the level for the Conditional Benefit would lie in the area between the lines BC and YC′. To the right of the point Y the additional revenue can be represented as a 'poll tax' equal to BX raised on all tax payers with Unadjusted Incomes greater than AY.

In the remainder of this appendix we will confine our attention to cases in which the Personal Tax Allowance under any Conditional Benefit regime is equal to the full Conditional Benefit of 1 unit. But it should be borne in mind that arrangements with a lower Personal Tax Allowance are possible and can introduce a very substantial alleviation of the budgetary problem.

We turn next to the consideration of Social Dividend regimes. Diagram 2 displays the hideous increase in excess expenditure which would be involved if the Conditional Benefit of Diagram 1 were simply turned into an unconditional Social Dividend without any increase in the rate of tax. The line ABC is repeated from Diagram 1 and shows the citizen's Adjusted Income under a Conditional Benefit, Personal Tax Allowance, and rate of tax which is assumed to balance the budget. The dashed line ADE now represents the Social Dividend regime. Every citizen receives the Social Dividend of OA and then on the whole of his or her Unadjusted Income pays a tax of 25 per cent so that the line ADE slopes up at 3 in 4 from the starting point A.

As a result of the change to the right of the points D and B, that is to say for all citizens whose Unadjusted Income exceeds 1 unit, every citizen receives as it were a 'poll-subsidy' equal to $\frac{3}{4}$ of a fully adequate standard of living of 1 unit, an amount which is measured by the excess of DE over BC.

This extra expense falls in the vertically hatched area { ||| } between DE and BC. Indeed for such citizens it is as if they received a full Personal Tax Allowance (MB) and in addition a fixed 'poll subsidy' (BD). This 'poll-subsidy' is equal to only $\frac{3}{4}$ of the Social Dividend because $\frac{1}{4}$ is in fact paid away in tax on the first unit of the citizen's Unadjusted Income.

This result can be clearly seen by extending the line CB until it cuts the vertical axis at the point marked A''. It can at once be seen that for all taxpayers to the right of M with Adjusted Incomes on the line BC it is quite indifferent whether the regime consists of a tax-free Personal Allowance equal to MB plus a tax of 25 per cent on all Unadjusted Income in excess of MB or whether the regime consists of a tax-free Social Dividend of OA'' plus a tax of 25 per cent on all Unadjusted Income without any tax-free Personal Allowance. The movement from the line BC to the higher line DE would in the latter case result simply from an increase in the Social Dividend of A''A = BD.

To the left of BD there will be some additional government expense on social benefits in the area ADB for those citizens (e.g. old age pensioners with some small income from capital or private pensions) who are already in receipt of Conditional Benefit.[14] There will, on the other hand, be some small offset in additional revenue in the triangle AJD due to tax paid on small earnings by persons who previously had no incentive to go out to work as long as their Conditional Benefit was reduced pound for pound, but now have some incentive to accept available low earnings of which they will retain 75 per cent.

It is patently clear from Diagram 2 that if the budget was balanced on the Conditional Benefit regime on the line ABC it would be hideously in deficit on the Social Dividend line ADE, if the rate of Income Tax were left unchanged at 25 per cent. One way of tackling this deficit would be to raise the rate of Income Tax, an adjustment which can be depicted by swinging the line ADE of Diagram 2 in a clockwise direction. The result of raising the rate from 25 per cent to 50 per cent is then shown in Diagram 3, where the line AD_1E_1 rises at a slope of 1 in 2 (since half of income is left untaxed) instead of the slope of 3 in 4 of Diagram 2.

With the regime of Diagram 3 all citizens to the right of point F (i.e. all citizens with Unadjusted Incomes greater than three times the Social Dividend) are worse off under the Social Dividend arrangement than they would have been under the Conditional Benefit regime of Diagram 1. What they gain in having a tax-free Social Dividend is more than offset by the higher rate of tax on their Unadjusted Incomes. From these citizens the State receives a net additional revenue in the horizontally hatched area between FC and FE_1 to the right of point F. To the left of point F citizens with positive Unadjusted Incomes gain more from the tax-free Social Dividend than they lose from the rise in the rate of tax; and the shift from the Conditional Benefit regime to the Social Dividend regime involves extra expenditure within the triangle AFB. For all citizens with zero Unadjusted Income (e.g. most children) there is no change in the State's expenditure. In the triangle AJD_1 there may be some moderate addition of revenue from the taxation of the low earnings of persons who under the Conditional Benefit regime had no incentive to work, but now seek work since they can retain 50 per cent of their pay.

Whether or not the raising of the rate of tax to 50 per cent would suffice to cover the cost of the Social Dividend scheme depends upon the distribution of the population of citizens along the Unadjusted Income horizontal axis. If there are many citizens to the right and few to the left of F, the additional revenue will be large relative to the additional expenditure. Among other factors this depends essentially upon the generosity of the level chosen for an adequate standard of living. If this basic unit of income was chosen to be equal to $\frac{1}{3}$ of the average Unadjusted Income per head of the population, there would lie as much income to the right of F producing a net excess of revenue over expenditure, as would lie to the left of F producing a net excess of expenditure over revenue.

Let us suppose that the Social Dividend regime of Diagram 3 with a 50 per cent rate of tax does balance the budget. Comparing the two regimes (the Social Dividend regime on line AD_1E_1 and the Conditional Benefit regime on line ABC) we can describe the difference as follows: both regimes start by giving the taxpayer 1 unit of income (he or she starts at point A instead of point O); the Social Dividend regime then taxes all additional income at 50 per cent; the Conditional Benefit regime then 'taxes' the first unit of additional income at 100 per cent and any further additional income at 25 per cent.

There is a second clear distinction between the effects of the two regimes. The Social Dividend regime has a much more marked equalising effect upon the distribution of Adjusted Incomes than does the Conditional Benefit regime. A shift from the latter to the former reduces the Adjusted Incomes of the better-off citizens to the right of F and raises the Adjusted Incomes of all the less well-off citizens to the left of F.

There is thus a stark choice between (i) a high degree of equalisation of standards, and a possible excessive degree of disincentives to work and enterprise from a Social Dividend regime with a 50 per cent marginal rate of tax on all Unadjusted Income and (ii) a markedly lower equalising effect combined with a reduction of the marginal rate of tax to 25 per cent on the vast majority of potential earners to the right of point M at the cost of a 100 per cent marginal rate of tax on those to the left of M.

There are, however, two types of regime which are, as it were, blends of Conditional Benefits and Social Dividends. They offer a possible selection of intermediate positions with equalising effects and marginal tax rate effects which lie between the two extremes presented by Conditional Benefit and Social Dividend regimes. The first possibility is to raise the rate of tax on the first unit of Unadjusted Income above the basic rate of tax on the rest of Unadjusted Income but without raising it to 100 per cent; this solution is depicted on Diagram 4. The second possibility is to pay a Social Dividend at a rate less than 1 unit (e.g. at a rate of 0.85 of an adequate standard of living) and to top this up to a fully adequate level by adding a Conditional Benefit (e.g. at a rate of 0.15) which will in turn be diminished pound for pound as the citizen receives any Unadjusted Income; this solution is illustrated in Diagram 5.

In Diagram 4 the line ABC represents once more the regime with a Conditional Benefit of 1 unit and a rate of income tax of 25 per cent, while the line AD_1E_1 is a reproduction of the line AD_1E_1 of Diagram 3 and represents the regime with a Social Dividend of 1 unit and a rate of income tax of 50 per cent. The line AD_2E_2 represents a Social Dividend regime in which the rate of income tax has been reduced from 50 per cent to 45 per cent, this reduction being offset by an additional Surcharge of 15 per cent on the first unit of each citizen's Unadjusted Income. Thus there is a combined levy of 60 per cent (45 per cent + 15 per cent) on the first unit of Unadjusted Income so that the line AD_2 rises at a slope of 2 in 5 (i.e. representing the 40 per cent of Unadjusted Income left after the combined tax of 60 per cent). From D_2 to E_2 the slope rises to 55 per cent, representing the proportion of income remaining after the tax of 45 per cent. It so happens that with this particular combination of Surcharge and reduced general rate of tax the D_1E_1 and D_2E_2 lines cut the BC line at the same point $F_{1,2}$, so that at a level of Unadjusted Income of 3 units a citizen would have the same standard of living under all three regimes.

With this change in Social Dividend regimes there would be a saving of State expenditure to the left of the point $F_{1,2}$ in the area between the lines $AD_1F_{1,2}$ and $AD_2F_{1,2}$ and there would be a reduction of State revenue to the right of point $F_{1,2}$ in the area between the lines $F_{1,2}E_2$ and $F_{1,2}E_1$. There is no reason to believe that this saving of expense would be exactly equal to the loss of revenue; whether or not this would be so depends upon the density of population at various points along the horizontal Unadjusted Income axis. But the imposition of a Surcharge on the first slice of Unadjusted Income can be a very powerful budgetary tool. It would certainly be possible to raise the Surcharge up to a level at which a 45 per cent general rate of tax would be sufficient to cover the cost of the Social Dividend scheme. At the extreme a Surcharge at a level which raised the combined rate of tax on the first unit of Unadjusted Income to 100 per cent would cause the AD_2 line to coincide with the AB line so that the general rate of tax could be reduced to 25 per cent on our assumption that such a rate would be sufficient to finance a Conditional Benefit of 1 unit.

Nor is it essential that the first slice of income on which a Surcharge is levied should be confined to the first unit of Unadjusted Income. The line AXE_3 in Diagram 4 represents a case in which (i) the general rate of tax is 45 per cent (as is the case of AD_2E_2), (ii) the Surcharge is 30 per cent causing a combined rate of tax of 75 per cent on the first slice of income, and (iii) the first slice of income on which surcharge is levied is raised from 1 unit to $1\frac{1}{3}$ units, this being the point at which the revenue from the combined rate of tax of 75 per cent on Unadjusted Income will just serve to repay the whole of the citizen's Social Dividend. By comparing the way in which the line AXE_3 lies below the line AD_2E_2 one can see how effective a Surcharge regime can be in raising revenue without raising the marginal rate of tax on the majority of taxpayers.

In Diagram 5 we turn to the other form of blend between Conditional Benefit and Social Dividend, namely an inadequate Social Dividend topped up by a reduced Conditional Benefit. We compare this new blend with the Surcharge regime which we have just discussed. Thus the line AD_2E_2 in Diagram 5 is simply a reproduction of the line AD_2E_2 of Diagram 4 and represents a regime with a Social Dividend of 1 unit combined with a 45 per cent rate of tax on all Unadjusted Income together with an additional Surcharge of 15 per cent on the first unit of Unadjusted Income. We compare this line with the line AGD_2E_2 which represents a regime with an inadequate Social Dividend of OH topped up by a Conditional Benefit of HA with a tax rate of 45 per cent on all Unadjusted Income without any Surcharge on the first unit of such income. We have chosen to set the new rate of Social Dividend at a level (OH = 0.85) which leaves all citizens to the right of the point D_2 in exactly the same position under both regimes. What they would lose from a reduction of Social Dividend from OA to OH they would gain by the removal of the Surcharge of 15 per cent on the first unit of their Unadjusted Income.

To the left of the point D_2, however, there is a marked change and the citizen's Adjusted Income is shown by the kinked line AGD_2 in place of the straight line AD_2. To the right of the point G the retention of 55 per cent of a citizen's Unadjusted Income more than makes up for the inadequacy (HA) of his or her Social Dividend and no supplementation of post-tax Unadjusted Income by Conditional Benefit is needed. But up to this point G, Conditional Benefit must be paid at a decreasing rate to supplement the deficiency of Social Dividend plus 55 per cent of Unadjusted Income.

Within the triangle AD_2G the budget would gain from saving on Social Dividend more than it lost on the elimination of the Surcharge; but this budgetary saving would be accompanied by some loss of revenue within the triangle AJK due to the discouragement of low earnings up to the point G. We assumed in the discussion of Diagram 4 that the budget can be balanced on the kinked line AD_2E_2. It follows, therefore, that if there were a net budgetary saving by choosing the regime AGD_2 instead of AD_2, it should be possible to finance a Social Dividend somewhat greater than OH. This possibility would, however, be very restricted. Any rise of the point H would cause the point D_2 on the AGD_2 regime to rise above the point D_2 on the line AD_2. This would represent a great loss of revenue equal to a corresponding 'poll-subsidy' to all the tax payers to the right of point D_2. In fact by choosing an adequate Social Dividend together with a Surcharge on the first unit of income instead of an inadequate Social Dividend together with

a Conditional Benefit but without any Surcharge one can improve the condition of the poorer members (in the triangle AD_2G) together with some
removal of disincentive to the lowest earners (in the triangle AJK) at the
expense, at the worst, of a very small additional 'poll tax' on the less needy
citizens.[15]

Diagrams 1 to 5 serve only to give a description of the structural features
of different institutional forms of Conditional Benefit, Social Dividend, and
Income Tax Regime. By observing along the horizontal axis the level of a
citizen's Unadjusted Income one can read off up the vertical axis what would
be the citizen's Adjusted Income after deduction of Income Tax and addition
of Conditional Benefit or Social Dividend. But this in itself gives no indication
of the total net budgetary revenue or expenditure resulting from the given
regime; that depends upon the number of citizens at each point of Unadjusted
Income.

In particular the diagrams in themselves say nothing about the direct effect
of the institution of any particular form of regime upon any particular
citizen's Unadjusted Income. The institution of a particular regime may well
cause a citizen to change his or her so-called Unadjusted Income before it is
subject to the Tax-Benefit Adjustments depicted in the relevant diagram.
Such changes in a citizen's so-called Unadjusted Income are likely to be most
pronounced under the straight-forward Social Dividend scheme of Diagram
3. In that regime the citizen is given a fully adequate fixed tax-free Social
Dividend, the receipt of which will make him or her have a less urgent need
to earn additional income. Moreover, for all better-off citizens this substantial
fixed income will be combined with a high marginal rate of tax on any
additional earnings and this increases the effort required to obtain any given
level of post-tax spendable income. The Social Dividend reduces the need for
additional spendable income and the higher rate of tax increases the cost of
obtaining additional spendable income. Together the two changes will lead
to a disincentive to earn additional income. This disincentive will cause the
citizen to produce a lower level of so-called Unadjusted Income before it is
subject to the particular Tax-Benefit regime of Diagram 3. Each such citizen
will have a lower so-called Unadjusted Income and will be subject to less tax
than would otherwise have been the case.

In discussion of Diagrams 1 to 5 no reference was made to these possible
disincentive effects of the different schemes. The only incentive effects to which
reference was made were the encouragement which a shift from Conditional
Benefits to some form of Social Dividend might give to citizens at the lower
end of the income scale to go out to earn a low income. In such cases the
scheme might lead to some improved incentives and so to some increased
earnings and increased budgetary tax revenue. But for the great majority of
citizens the various Social Dividend schemes are liable to cause substantial
disincentive effects leading to a substantial reduction of governmental
revenue. In comparing the pure Social Dividend scheme of Diagram 3 with
the pure Conditional Benefit scheme of Diagram 1 we assumed for purely
illustrative purposes that there would be a need for a rise in the rate of tax
from 25 per cent to 50 per cent. Some part of this rise in rate of tax must be

attributed to the disincentive effects leading to a reduction in the total level of taxable incomes.

There is a second set of factors affecting incentives and disincentives which must be borne in mind. Diagrams 1 to 5 are all drawn on the assumption that it is total Unadjusted Income which is subject to Income Tax. But in Part III of the main text it is suggested that the basis of tax should not be total Unadjusted Income (U) but only Unadjusted Income less net Savings (U–S). Diagrams 1 to 5 can then remain unchanged if we measure (U–S) instead of U along the horizontal axis. The corresponding height up the vertical axis will then measure the citizens expenditure on consumption (C).[16]

The exemption of savings from Income Tax will of course reduce the revenue raised in tax in all cases in which citizens are saving any part of their income. We have assumed in Part III of the main text that this loss of revenue is made good by additional taxation on wealth or on the transfer of wealth by gift or bequest. But how much lost revenue from Income Tax must be replaced by additional revenue from Capital Taxation will depend not only upon the level of savings which would have occurred if savings had not been exempt from tax, but also upon any effects of the exemption of savings from tax on the incentive of citizens to earn more or less income or to save more or less out of any given income. It is not possible in this simple appendix to consider in detail the nature or extent of these possible secondary incentive effects of the introduction of exemption of savings from tax. But in general there is no reason to believe that they will be very great in one direction or the other in the case of the better-off citizens.

But at the bottom end of the scale there is one important effect to be noted. The exemption of savings from tax means that any citizen who earns more and saves all the additional Unadjusted Income will not pay any additional tax; and as depicted in the Diagrams this result is true of the lowest incomes even under a Conditional Benefit scheme. The level of income OA in Diagram 1 is the Conditional Benefit which will be paid at the origin O when U–S, and not necessarily U, is zero. So long as a citizen consumes no more than OA (i.e. saves all his or her Unadjusted Income and lives only on the Conditional Benefit OA), the citizen will continue to receive this unchanged amount of Conditional Benefit. All citizens however low their earnings have, even under a Conditional Benefit scheme, some incentive to earn since they can without any loss of consumption save the whole of those earnings with the intention of building up their Unadjusted Income until it exceeds OA. From this point on they will be in a position to use part of their Unadjusted Income in order to raise their level of consumption, any excess of Unadjusted Income over the basic level of OA being subject only to the general rate of Income Tax even if none of it is saved.

For this reason there will be a very strong incentive indeed under a Conditional Benefit scheme for the whole of low earnings to be saved, since otherwise they will be 'taxed' 100 per cent by an equivalent reduction of the Conditional Benefit. There will be a strong, though somewhat less decisive, incentive under the Surcharge scheme of Diagram 4 for any low incomes to be saved. Any such savings will exempt the saver of low income from the

Surcharge as well as the general tax rate on all such savings; but the prospective yield on such savings will be taxed only at the general rate of tax if
it is spent later when the saver has built up his or her income to a level above
the basic Social Dividend level. If it is desired to promote the equalisation of
the ownership of wealth by promoting the savings of those with little property
while taxing the wealth of those with much property, the effects of a Conditional Benefit scheme or Social Dividend cum Surcharge scheme under a
Savings exempt Income Tax regime should be borne in mind.[17]
   In Diagrams 1, 3, 4 and 5 we have depicted the following five regimes:

Regime 1   A Conditional Benefit of 1 unit with a Rate of Income Tax of 25
         per cent on the line ABC.
Regime 3   A Social Dividend of 1 unit with a Rate of Income Tax of 50 per
         cent on the line AE_1.
Regime 4   A Social Dividend of 1 unit with a Rate of Income Tax of 45 per
         cent plus a 15 per cent Surcharge on the first unit of Unadjusted
         Income on the line AD_2E_2.
Regime 5   A Social Dividend of 0.85 of a unit with a Conditional Benefit of
         0.15 of a unit and a Rate of Income Tax of 45 per cent on the line
         AGD_2E_2.

All these Regimes are assumed to be such as will preserve a balanced
governmental budget without any change in other governmental taxes or
expenditures.
   One may summarise the relative merits and demerits of these various
forms of Social Benefit or Social Dividend schemes under the following four
headings:

   (1)   Incentive Effects
   (2)   Redistributive Effects
   (3)   Risk-Bearing Effects
   (4)   Administrative problems

(1)   Incentive Effects

The different schemes have very different incentive effects at the top and the
bottom ends of the income scale. Regime 1 has the least disincentive effects
at the top end of the scale where it provides what corresponds to a Social
Dividend of only OA″ in size (see Diagram 2) combined with a low marginal
rate of tax of 25 per cent. But it has the greatest possible disincentive effects
at the bottom end of the scale where it threatens to tax away 100 per cent of
all earnings. At the other extreme Regime 3 has the worst disincentive effects
at the top end of the scale with a high Social Dividend of OA combined with
the highest marginal rate of tax of 50 per cent; but it has the least unfavourable
disincentive effects at the bottom end of the scale. Regime 4 is a compromise,
reducing moderately the disincentives of Regime 3 at the top end and those
of Regime 1 at the bottom end of the income scale. Regime 5 has the same

disincentive effects as Regime 4 for those at the top end of the scale and it extends these moderate disincentive effects further down the income scale (over the range GB in Diagram 5); but this it does at the expense of re-introducing the absolute disincentives of Regime 1 for those at the very bottom of the income scale (over the range AG in Diagram 5).

This summary needs some modification if one is dealing with an Income Tax Regime which exempts savings from tax. In particular the absolute or heavy disincentives at the bottom of the scale in Regimes 1, 4 and 5 will be modified in that any income which is earned will escape the excessive marginal rates of tax of 100 per cent or of general rate plus surcharge if the income is saved.

(2)   Redistributive Effects

The redistributive effects of Regime 1 can be very great. They consist of raising sufficient revenue at the expense of all those above OM on the income scale in order to raise up to the level OA the incomes of all those with incomes below OA, as can be seen in Diagram 1. All the other regimes have even greater redistributive effects than Regime 1. The excess redistributive effects of Regimes 3 and 4 can be seen from Diagram 4 where the distribution of Adjusted Income is represented by the line ABC for Regime 1, by AD_1E_1 for Regime 3, and AD_2E_2 for Regime 4.

Both Regime 3 and Regime 4 have greater redistributive effect than Regime 1 since in both cases those to the right of point F are worse off than with Regime 1 while those to the left of F (other than those clustered at the origin with zero Unadjusted Incomes) are all better off than with Regime 1. But the redistribution effect of Regime 3 is greater than that of Regime 4 since those to the right of point F are better off while those to the left of F are worse off with Regime 4 than with Regime 3. Regime 5 has substantially the same overall redistributive effect as Regime 4 except that with Regime 5 those near the bottom of the income scale are likely to fare somewhat less well.

(3)   Risk-Bearing Effects

There remains the argument in favour of a Social Dividend scheme that it will make it more acceptable for workers to accept partnership arrangements under which their earnings will vary with the fortunes of the partnership enterprise, if they have some element of fixed income to fall back on. A Social Dividend certainly has an effect of this kind but the effect is a limited one. Its extent is illustrated by the figures in Table 4.

In considering the results shown in Table 4 there are two factors to be taken into account. If a citizen's Unadjusted Income falls by 10 per cent there are two ways in which the impact on the Adjusted Income will be mitigated. In the first place, the greater the ratio of the fixed Social Dividend to his or her other income, the smaller will be the percentage fall in his or her Adjusted Income. In the second place, the higher the marginal rate of tax, the greater

TABLE 4 THE PERCENTAGE FALL IN A CITIZEN'S ADJUSTED
INCOME RESULTING FROM A 10 PER CENT DECLINE IN UNAD-
JUSTED INCOME

Level of Unadjusted Income	0.5	2	4
Regime 1	Nil	8.6	9.2
Regime 3	2.0	5.0	6.7
Regime 4	1.8	5.6	7.3
Regime 5	2.4		

the amount of any loss of pre-tax income which is absorbed by paying a smaller amount of tax to the government. Thus for all income above the basic standard level of unity, the percentage fall in Adjusted Income is smaller (i) the nearer the Unadjusted Income approaches unity (since the fixed Social Dividend becomes a larger proportion of total income as one moves from income 4 to income 2), (ii) the higher the marginal rate of tax (as one moves from Regime 1 through Regimes 4 or 5 to Regime 3), and (iii) the higher the Social Dividend (as one moves to Regimes 3, 4 and 5 from Regime 1 with its low 'notional' social Dividend of OA'' as shown on Diagram 2). Below unit income the risk depends upon the structure of the Regime. It is totally absorbed by the government's adjustment of Conditional Benefit in Regime 1. It is absorbed by tax plus surcharge in Regime 4 and by tax alone without Surcharge in Regime 3 and by a still lower rate of tax in Regime 5. But if Unadjusted Income were $\frac{1}{4}$ or less, the relevant rate of tax for Regime 5 would rise to 100 per cent and the whole of the fall in Unadjusted Income would be absorbed by tax as in Regime 1.

(4)   Administrative Problems

If Conditional Benefits depend solely upon a citizen's Unadjusted Income (as is the case in all the Regimes discussed in the appendix) there are no administrative problems concerned with the determination whether a citizen is sick, involuntarily unemployed, etc. The one determining factor is the level of his or her Unadjusted Income.

   If, however, the Income Tax Regime is one which exempts net Savings from tax, it will be essential to assess Unadjusted Income and Savings separately for each individual citizen. The kinks in tax liability at the level OM in Regimes 1 and 4 and at the level AG in Regime 5 could raise additional administrative tasks. For this reason the pure Social Dividend Regime 3 would be administratively the simplest. Indeed if the Income Tax Regime did not exempt Savings and if the rate of tax were constant at 50 per cent over all ranges of Unadjusted Income there would be no need for individual assessment. The administrative problem would be simply to pay the fixed Social Dividend to all citizens and to raise, at source if possible, a 50 per cent rate of tax on all Unadjusted Income.

The best way to summarise the main points is as follows. The higher the Social Dividend and the higher the general rate of tax imposed to finance it, the greater will be the beneficial effects on the equalisation of Adjusted Incomes and on the mitigation of risk-bearing. But both the rise in the Social Dividend (which enables people to enjoy a given income without earning so much) and the higher marginal rate of tax (which reduces the net return on any additional earnings) will tend to reduce economic incentives for work and enterprise. In the choice of policies these results must be weighed against each other.

Diagrams

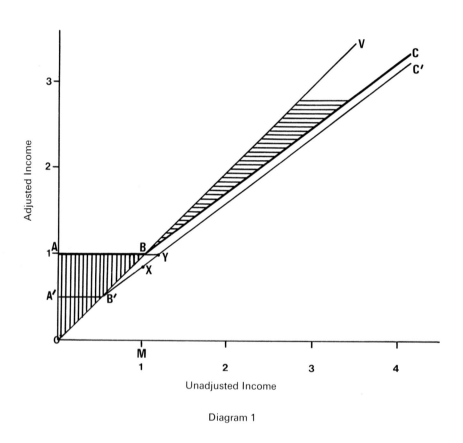

Diagram 1

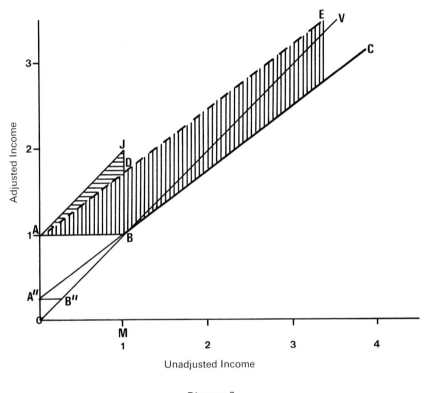

Diagram 2

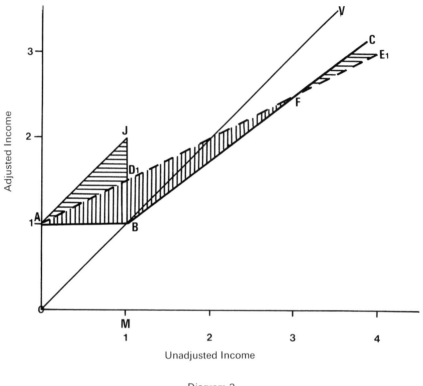

Diagram 3

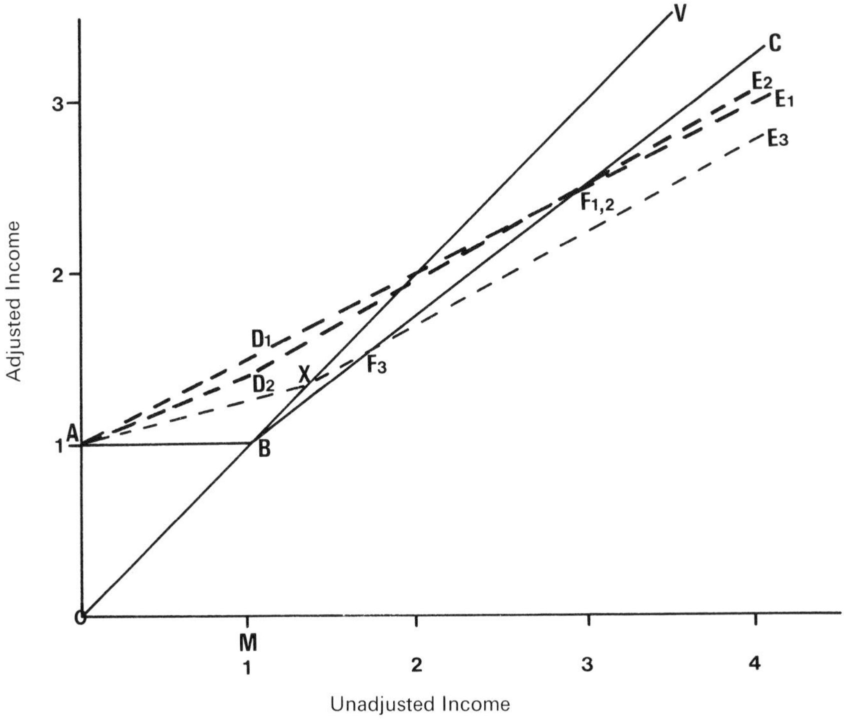
V
C
E2
E1
E3
F1,2
D1
D2
X
F3
A
B
O
M
1
2
3
4
1
2
3
Adjusted Income
Unadjusted Income

Diagram 4

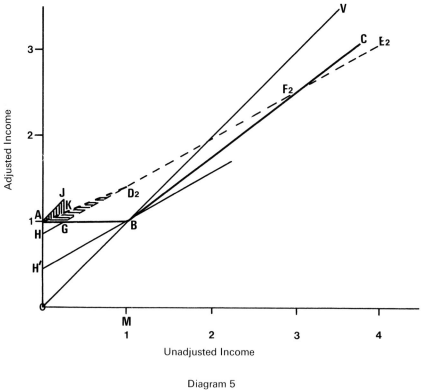

Diagram 5

Notes

1.   Part II of the present tract is a revised and much enlarged version of Chapter VI of my book *Alternative Systems of Business Organisation and of Workers' Remuneration* (Allen and Unwin, 1986) and of Section 7 of my pamphlet 'Different Forms of Share Economy' (Public Policy Centre, London, 1986). Part III is a revised and much enlarged version of the paper which was presented at the afternoon session of the Rome conference.

2.   Published by Giangiacomo Feltrinelli Editore, Milan, 1989.

3.   In economists' jargon it can be noted that the discussion in the text is about the relationship between a factor's cost and its marginal revenue product, and not about the relationship between its cost and the value of its marginal product.

4.   Or perhaps not quite the best of all possible arrangements. Agathotopia (the Good Place) is only one of the group of Topian Islands which includes also Ameinotopia (the Better Place), Aristotopia (the Best Possible Place), Utopia (the Non-existent Perfect Place) and, beyond Utopia, Cacotopia (the Bad Place), Caciōtopia (the Worse Place) and Cacistotopia (the Worst Place). There is great excitement among the Topians because the Utopians have suggested that they introduce a common currency and harmonise their rates of tax. Many Agathotopians including my old friend Professor Dr Semaj Edaem, are very worried as to how far they can go without endangering the survival of the rather distinctive Agathotopian economic institutions and policies.

5.   See Theodor Hertzka, *Freeland, A Social Anticipation* (Chatto and Windus, London, 1891).

6.   See Professor Mario Nuti, 'On Traditional Cooperatives and James Meade's Labour-Capital Discriminating Partnerships'. Paper presented at a Conference of the Lega Nazionale delle Cooperative e Mutue, Rome, March 1988.

7.   At the other extreme of a concern's life, namely on the voluntary liquidation of a partnership, conflict can well once more emerge. In the case of a large concern with many capitalist shareholders it is practicable to rule that voluntary liquidation should be arranged only with the agreement of the majority of worker partners as well as of the majority of capitalist partners. In this case there would have to be some reasonable agreed treatment of the interests of the worker partners. But in the case of, for example, a one-man capitalist setting up a retail shop and taking on assistants as worker partners endowed with Labour Share Certificates, it would be unreasonable—indeed perhaps impracticable—for the worker partners to be able to prevent the one-man owner from retiring and taking his capital out of the business. The Agathotopians seek for such cases some rule which requires the capitalist partner on liquidation of the business to devote some share of the value of the concern's assets to the compensation of the worker partners.

[8] In Appendix A the factors affecting the restrictive forces due to the rules of redistribution and of cancellation are discussed and illustrated in greater detail.

[9] Cf. Maurice Allais. Chapter IV.1 of L'Impôt sur le Capital et La Réforme Monetaire. *Hermann Editeur* (Paris, 1977).

[10] The characteristics of the various Social Dividend schemes are discussed in greater detail in Appendix B at the end of the main text.

[11] This method of dealing with the problem has been suggested to Professor Semaj Edaem by Mr Martin Weale of Cambridge University. See also Chapter 12 of the report on 'The Structure and Reform of Direct Taxation' by a committee set up by the Institute for Fiscal Studies (Allen and Unwin, 1978).

[12] If $\sigma = 0$ and the whole of the pure profit of a retiring worker partner is distributed among the remaining worker partners, in the form of an equal distribution among them of the number of shares of the retiring number which are not needed to meet the cost of living of the new replacement worker, the distribution shown in the table is precisely accurate. But if $\sigma = \bar{\sigma}$ the distribution of the benefit of $B(1-\bar{\sigma})$ among the remaining $m-1$ partners will not be strictly equal at $B(1-\bar{\sigma})/(m-1)$. This is so because the distribution of benefit will now take place not by a distribution of an equal number of Share Certificates to all remaining worker partners (as with the rule of redistribution), but instead (as with the rule of cancellation) by rise in the rate of dividend on all Share Certificates of which a proportion $B\bar{\sigma}$ will go to the holders of Capital Share Certificates. The remaining proportion $B(1-\bar{\sigma})$ will be distributed among the existing worker partners not equally, but in proportion to their holdings of Labour Share Certificates. One team of these partners (namely the newly engaged team m of Year 1) will hold fewer Share Certificates (only enough to cover their cost) than the other remaining $m-2$ teams of Year 1 which will hold an additional number of shares corresponding to their pure profit. The $B\mu_1$ of Year 2 should in this case be somewhat larger. This inaccuracy will be of importance only in those cases in which pure profit is large relatively to cost.

[13] For purposes of simplicity of algebraic exposition the story of a contraction of workers' membership has been told in terms of the non-replacement of one whole team. But in fact the restriction would probably take the more gradual form of a reduction in the number engaged in each individual team as it was replaced. In any resulting steady state one could once again reach a new situation in which there were m teams with each team being smaller in number so that $\bar{B}/W$ would be higher and could satisfy the critical condition indicated in (5).

[14] If x is a citizen's Unadjusted Income in this range the state pays $1-x$ under the Conditional Benefit Scheme. With the Social Dividend scheme the State pays 1 unit in Social Dividend but receives in tax tx, a net charge to the State of $1-tx$. The additional charge to the State is thus $(1-tx)-(1-x) = x(1-t)$.

[15] In Diagram 5 the line H'B is drawn parallel to the line HD$_2$ and thus measures what a citizen's Adjusted Income would be with a Social Dividend of OH' and a tax rate of 45 per cent. It is clear that for the point G to lie to the left of the point B any Social Dividend must be greater than OH'. In other words in order that an inadequate Social Dividend should help to relieve pressure on the payment of Conditional Benefit it must exceed OH', which corresponds to the value at the general rate of income tax of a Personal Tax Allowance (OM) which is equal to the Conditional Benefit (MB).

[16] If U = Unadjusted Income, D = Social Dividend, B = Conditional Benefit and T = Total paid in tax, the amount available to the Citizen to spend or save (i.e. C+S) must be equal to U+D+B−T. Thus

$$C = U - S + D + B - T.$$

If the basis of tax is $U - S$, $T = t(U - S)$, so that

$$(U - S)(1 - t) + D + B = C,$$

which is what is measured up the vertical axis in each diagram, when $(U - S)$ is measured along the horizontal axis. When $U = S$, i.e. at the point O on the horizontal axis, we will have $C = D + B$. So that D or B measures the level of consumption which is attainable if the whole of the unadjusted income is saved.

[17] The Diagrams 1 to 5 do not indicate what would happen if $U < S$, so that $U - S$ were negative. The diagrams cover all the cases in which $U - S$ is zero or greater than zero. A situation in which $U - S$ were negative would be one in which a citizen was saving more than his or her total Unadjusted Income, i.e. was saving part of his or her Conditional Benefit or Social Dividend. Consumption would fall below the basic adequate level unless D or B were raised to cover the excess saving.

THE DAVID HUME INSTITUTE

The David Hume Institute was established as a company limited by guarantee in January 1985, and it is registered as a charity. Its registration number in Scotland is 91239.

The objects of the Institute are to promote discourse and research on the economic and legal aspects of public policy questions.

Honorary President (1988–1991) Judge Thijmen Koopmans, Court of Justice of the European Communities
Chairman Sir Gerald Elliot FRSE
Executive Director Professor Sir Alan Peacock FBA
Secretary and Treasurer H L Snaith

21 George Square
Edinburgh EH8 9LD
Tel: 031 667 7004

HUME PAPERS
1   Banking Deregulation *Michael Fry*
2   Reviewing Industrial Aid Programmes:
    (1) The Invergordon Smelter Case *Alex Scott and Margaret Cuthbert*
3   Sex at Work: Equal Pay and the "Comparable Worth" Controversy *Peter Sloane*
4   The European Communities' Common Fisheries Policy: A Critique *Antony W Dnes*
5   The Privatisation of Defence Supplies *Gavin Kennedy*
6   The Political Economy of Tax Evasion *David J Pyle*
7   Monopolies, Mergers and Restrictive Practices: UK Competition Policy 1948–87 *E Victor Morgan*

Published by **Aberdeen University Press**
8   The Small Entrepreneurial Firm *Gavin C Reid and Lowell R Jacobsen*
9   How Should Health Services be Financed? *Allan Massie*
10 Strategies for Higher Education—The Alternative White Paper *John Barnes and Nicholas Barr*
11 Professional Liability *Roger Bowles and Philip Jones*
12 Deregulation and the Future of Commercial Television *Gordon Hughes and David Vines*
13 The Ethics of Business *Norman Barry*
14 Intellectual Copyright *Hector MacQueen*
15 Student Loans *Nicholas Barr*
16 Agathotopia: The Economics of Partnership *James E Meade*